The Torment
of Buddy Rich

The Torment of Buddy Rich

A Biography

First Edition

John Minahan

Writer's Showcase
presented by *Writer's Digest*
San Jose New York Lincoln Shanghai

The Torment of Buddy Rich
A Biography

Writer's Showcase
presented by *Writer's Digest*
an imprint of iUniverse.com, Inc.

For information address:
iUniverse.com, Inc.
5220 S 16th, Ste. 200
Lincoln, NE 68512
www.iuniverse.com

Grateful acknowledgment is made to American Airlines for permission
to reprint the article, "Buddy Rich: One of a Kind," by Mel Tormé,
from the December, 1974, issue of *The American Way* magazine,
copyright (c) 1974 by The American Way. Reprinted with permission.

ISBN: 0-595-13745-8

Printed in the United States of America

Also by John Minahan

A Sudden Silence
The Passing Strange
The Dream Collector
Jeremy
Sorcerer
Nine-Thirty-Fifty-Five
Almost Summer
Nunzio
Complete American Graffiti
Eyewitness
The Great Hotel Robbery
The Great Diamond Robbery
Mask
The Face Behind the Mask
The Great Pyramid Robbery
The Great Harvard Robbery
The Great Grave Robbery
The Quiet American
Forests of the Night

Translation

The Fabulous Onassis

Acknowledgments

I WANT TO express my appreciation for the active participation of the Rich family, including Buddy's father Bob, his brother Mickey, his sisters Margie and Jo, his wife Marie, and his daughter Cathy. A special note of gratitude goes to Stanley Kay, his longtime manager, for helping to put it all in perspective. My thanks also for the valuable insights provided by (in alphabetical order): Bobbi Arnstein, Count Basie, Paul Burke, Johnny Carson, Bob Cavallo, George Duvivier, Dizzie Gillespie, Lionel Hampton, Hugh Hefner, Woody Herman, Milt Hinton, Gerry Mulligan, Carl Palmer, Zoot Sims, Frank Sinatra, Mel Tormé, and Teddy Wilson.

J.M.

This book is dedicated to
STANLEY KAY,
one of the few honest men I've ever known.

Take a good look at the man. He'll probably be around as long as me, maybe longer. But just in case he isn't, take a good look, and don't forget what you saw.

COUNT BASIE
(in conversation)

Foreword

BUDDY RICH ONCE told me that he was the loneliest man in the universe. We were alone in his dressing room upstairs at Buddy's Place, his new club in New York, the year was 1974, and he had just finished a frenzied session of slamming his fists into the two karate punching pads on the wall. When he said it, he was sweating and out of breath and one of his knuckles was bleeding.

He didn't have to explain what he meant. It was understood. You had clues even the first time you met him, talked with him, saw him play. The vibrations were just so strong you couldn't possibly miss them. He was an extremely angry man, screaming inside himself. If he didn't explode at something or somebody on a fairly consistent basis, I think he probably would have blown his brains out.

If personality can be defined as the visible aspect of an individual's character, as it impresses others, then there was something intuitively dangerous about him. You knew it when you saw it. Not that he seemed to threaten you. It was just a gut reaction. A caution light went on in the mind.

The anger and loneliness had relatively little to do with his friends or family. To get anywhere near the root cause of what made Buddy so obviously different from most of us, you have to go back more than eighty years to vaudeville in its heyday. We were racing into Scott Fitzgerald's 1920s, movies were flickering with silent Chaplins, Swansons, and Valentinos, jazz was finally moving up-river from New Orleans to Chicago, and Buddy Rich was making his debut as a drummer in his parents' vaudeville act, playing the best national circuits. He was eighteen months old when he played *Stars and Stripes Forever* before his first audience.

He became a permanent part of the act when he was three. At seven, he was a single, touring theaters in the United States and Australia. Billed as "Traps," the drum wonder, he became the second highest paid child star in the world, topped only by Jackie Coogan. After several particularly dazzling stints on Broadway, his reputation as a drummer had become so widespread that a top national drum manufacturer asked him to endorse a new line of drums.

"Traps," the boy phenomenon, flourished for seven very lucrative years before the Rich family—parents and all four children—retired from vaudeville and settled comfortably in Brooklyn, New York. Buddy was fourteen. The damage had been done. He had received virtually no formal education, no training in anything but the drums, and had long since begun to withdraw into himself, feeling a deep sense of inferiority among others his age..

His options were extremely limited—and he knew it only too well. In retrospect, Buddy believed this was probably the initial catalyst for the isolation and anger that would follow and build. "I'm a drummer because I had no *choice*," he told me. "What the hell else could I do? I could barely read and write."

Jazz had been moving from Chicago to Kansas City and on to New York, and Buddy began studying the serious jazz drummers, with a preference for Chick Webb, Baby Dodds, Joe Jones, and Dave Tough. His first break as a jazz drummer came in 1938 when he was offered a job with Joe Marsala's band at New York's famed Hickory House. He remained a year, then played briefly with Bunny Berigan, then put in two years with Artie Shaw. When he finally moved up to the Tommy Dorsey

Orchestra, his career was interrupted by World War II; he served with the U.S. Marines, 1942–44.

After discharge, Buddy rejoined the Dorsey group, became the highest-paid sideman in the business, and made swing-era history. The recordings of *I'll Take Tallullah, Not So Quiet, Please,* and *Hawaiian War Chant* became classics, and it was during these years that Buddy earned the title "World's Greatest Drummer."

While with the Dorsey band, Buddy roomed with Frank Sinatra, and, although their feuds sometimes made front-page news, it was Sinatra who backed Buddy's first band after they both left Dorsey. Unfortunately, big bands were already in decline, and Buddy's lasted only five years.

Harry James formed an exciting band in the early 1960s and Buddy joined at an unprecedented $1,500 a week, regaining the status of highest-paid sideman until he left in 1966 to lead his own band again.

During the next two decades, his bright young group of sixteen men traveled the world playing theaters, concert halls, festivals, colleges, and the modern caverns of light and sound. He played the music of today, distinctively Rich, with no bending in any direction. Almost to the end (he died of a brain tumor, April 2, 1987), you had to literally see the man in action to believe the sound, speed, dexterity, and virtuosity.

Very few of us will ever know the satisfaction of even coming close to being number one in our professions; in music, the odds are astronomical. Musicologists tell us that in the ideal—or abstract—situation, an individual is genetically predisposed with a special talent, works at it from infancy, isolated from distractions and denied any choice in the matter, until the discipline develops into an almost monomaniacal drive for perfection.

Buddy Rich achieved that perfection. The cost was very high.

This book was written in the form of a diary, researched as I traveled with Buddy to various cities in the U.S., Canada, England, and Scotland. It was not intended to be an authoritative analysis of an eminent contemporary musician or a detailed biographical treatment. It is a selective account of representative events in the life of a musical genius, an attempt to reflect aspects of his complex personality and the role played by his family, friends, and enemies—real and imagined.

In this connection, we have the advantage of listening to some of his oldest friends, business associates, and musicians, as well as his detractors, men and women who candidly discuss subjects ranging from his childhood to his sixties, and they are all asked the hard questions, the questions that often they alone can answer.

In researching this book, a conscious effort was made to achieve balance, perspective, and proportion, to reveal the man and his work as honestly as possible, warts and all, no punches pulled. Every interview was tape recorded and transcribed verbatim to ensure accuracy, and every historical fact and figure was documented by a variety of sources.

What emerges from all this is an unusual life story as well as an extraordinary love story. When you enter the world of Buddy Rich, you should be warned that there are few conventional road signs to indicate that you are in the presence of genius.

But you are.

I

THAT AFTERNOON WE had a window table in the upstairs dining room at DiLillo's on Fifty-third Street between Fifth and Sixth in Manhattan. It was a very popular Italian restaurant, but not crowded then at 3:30. Buddy Rich was half an hour late. Stanley Kay kept glancing at his watch and drumming his knife on the tablecloth. Stanley was fifty that year, a lean, serious guy with steel-gray hair, white at the temples. Buddy's attorney, Bob Cavallo, adjusted his glasses as he read *Newsweek*, thick dark hair, banker's-gray suit, in his early forties, a guy with a quick and easy sense of humor. I sipped my iced coffee and looked down at the crowded sidewalk, garbage cans overflowing at the curbs, cars and taxis and trucks jammed four-abreast, bumper-to-bumper, horns blowing, the usual. The day was Thursday, July 11, 1974.

Stanley checked his watch again. "Something must've happened."

Bob glanced up from his magazine, adjusted his glasses. He had the kind of self-assured attitude that inspired confidence in a courtroom, but his voice sometimes changed unexpectedly, as if in adolescence. "There's a very simple explanation," he told us. "Very simple. Some poor bastard looked crooked at him on the street and got his head busted. Karate shot to the temple. Very clean. Very fast. Like those boards he breaks. Now he's being booked for manslaughter. Our defense? Insanity. Not just temporary insanity. Permanent, total, congenital, out-and-out bananas insanity."

Stanley smiled, but he wasn't in the mood. "No, see, that's the thing about B. He's never late. I mean, you know that. All right, he worked last night, he probably didn't get to bed till four or five. But that don't mean nothing with him. I mean, I've known the man for thirty-five years."

Bob looked at him. "Stanley."

"No, that's straight."

"Stanley, cut the shit, huh?"

"No, I'm telling you, it's a fetish with him."

Bob handed the copy of *Newsweek* to me, opened to an article about the New York Jazz Festival. There was a good picture of Buddy with Lionel Hampton. One of the final paragraphs was intriguing to me:

> But if you had to single out one performance, it had to be the quartet of Lionel Hampton, Buddy Rich, Teddy Wilson and bassist Milt Hinton. They typified the festival, looking back as well as forward. Old hands, they played like new ones, with the integration and the elegance of a classical quartet. Hampton made some of the loveliest sounds heard all week long, and from the first bars of "Avalon" he and Buddy Rich played cat-and-mouse, daring each other into ever more playful explorations.

"That whole festival was dynamite," Stanley said. "Blues, ragtime, Dixieland, swing, bop, pop, jam, they had it all. Dizzy— you hear the number Dizzy pulled? They were interviewing him, some newspaper guys, I don't know. One young cat, he comes up to him, he says, 'Mr. Gillespie, how would you define bop?' Well, Dizzie, he gives him a look, you know? Says, 'Bop. Bop. How would I define bop?' He thinks about it, he's frowning, holding his forehead, the whole number. So then he straightens up, he clears his throat, they got their pencils and pads all ready, right? He says,

'Well, actually, what it is,' he says, 'I mean what it *was*—well, see, we just stole some tunes.'"

We laughed. Stanley had the accent down cold.

"'We just stole some tunes,'" he said, laughing, savoring it.

We talked about Buddy for a while, and how, at fifty-six, he was actually becoming more popular than he had ever been in his long career.

A short time later, when Buddy finally arrived, he walked toward us at a fast clip, staring straight ahead, and it was obvious by his face and posture that he was very angry. He didn't look fifty-six back then, nowhere near it, full head of dark hair, modern aviator-style glasses, body lean and hard and almost athletic in a tight white turtleneck and jeans, but his face had some mileage.

"What happened?" Stanley asked.

Buddy sat down, leaned forward stiffly, clenched his hands tightly together on the table, stared at them. He took a couple of deep breaths.

"What, somebody downstairs?" Stanley asked.

"The motherfuckin' *cabbie*," he snapped, trying to keep his voice low. "The cocksucker shouldn't be *driving* a cab, he shouldn't be *allowed* in a cab!"

"What'd he do?" I asked.

"Three-fifteen in the afternoon and he can't change a twenty-dollar bill! Can't change a *twenty*! I have to get out, I have to go in to the cashier in the *restaurant*—and then *he* gives me an argument!"

"Oh, man," Stanley said.

The light bulb in a fixture directly above his head started to flicker. It may have been doing that before he arrived, but I didn't notice.

Buddy glanced up at it, then concentrated on his hands again. "The fare is two dollars and thirty cents. I go in, I get change, I come out, I give him exactly two dollars and thirty cents. Period.

No tip, no nothing. So he tries to do a number on me. I told him exactly what he could do. I told him to go take a flyin' *fuck*!"

In the pause, we could hear soft music and the voice of a radio disk jockey. Buddy stared at his clenched hands. The light bulb above his head went completely out, then flickered on again.

Buddy glanced up at it, then at Stanley, kept his voice low. "If somebody doesn't fix that fuckin' thing right *now*, I'm walking out of here."

Stanley stood up quickly and left the table.

"The start of another sunny day," Bob said softly.

I remember how Buddy's face reacted first, eyes and mouth closing tightly, as if in pain. Then his shoulders started shaking and he was laughing through his nose, and in another few seconds his head went down on the table and his whole body was shaking with laughter. Bob and I started laughing too, more in relief than anything else. Buddy tried several times to say something, couldn't get it out, and all of us were howling by then. As I look back on it, I don't think I had ever seen a man change moods so quickly from one extreme to another.

Stanley came back with a short man carrying a stepladder. For some reason, just seeing them together broke up Buddy and Bob. Stanley accepted the whole change of mood as if it were an everyday occurrence. He made the transition immediately, imitated a vaudeville MC, introduced the short man as "Ladders LaRue" and announced that he'd now do his act for us—"Screwin' Light Bulbs." We all applauded. The short guy just stood there uncertainly, with a half-smile, probably thinking we were all bombed. Then Stanley put his arm around him, all apologies, and the little guy changed the light bulb in record time.

Before lunch arrived, the radio music changed to a news broadcast. We didn't pay much attention to it until somebody heard the name "Frank Sinatra," then Buddy wanted to listen. That week,

Sinatra's latest scuffle with the press happened in Australia on his world concert tour and each episode was widely publicized. First, Old Blue Eyes' bodyguards roughed up some photographers. Next, he announced from the stage in Melbourne that reporters were "bums" and referred to newswomen as "hookers." Now Australia's in a national uproar. Outraged musicians, stagehands, and other union members rush to the support of the Australian Journalists' Association. Sinatra and his group are refused all kinds of services, including fuel for their private jet. One concert has to be canceled. President of the Australian Council of Trade Unions says flatly, "He'll never get out of the country until he apologizes." Finally, a joint statement is released, saying that Sinatra meant no moral reflection on Australian journalists, but he reserves the right to criticize individuals. There's no apology for anything. Embargo's lifted, tour continues. As the world turns. Newscaster turns to another subject.

Buddy clapped his hands, looked happy. "Apologize! Oh, yeah, that'll be the day. That'll be *the* day when Frank apologizes to *those* assholes."

"That's his man," Stanley told me. "Frank and him were room-mates, with the Dorsey band."

Bob touched Buddy's arm. "Tell him about *your* tour there in 'sixty-seven."

He nodded, cleared his throat, took a deep breath with his teeth clenched. "This'll give you an idea of the mentality of these people Frank's dealing with down there. I took the big band on a concert tour of Australia in nineteen sixty-seven. We were in Tasmania for one day, we did a television show, we were leaving for Melbourne next morning. So we had this suite in the hotel. Leo and I had a twin-bedded room and Cathy—"

"Leo's his secretary," Stanley told me.

"Right, and Cathy was with us, my daughter, she had her own room. Okay, we turned in, we were all asleep. I don't know what time it was, two, three o'clock in the morning, we heard this knocking at the front door. Y'know, nothing timid—very, very authoritative. Bam-bam-bam-bam-bam! Leo jumped out of bed; I just opened my eyes. Next thing, I hear Leo rapping with somebody about something, and I called out, 'What is it?' He said, 'Please come out, Buddy.' So I did. I put on a robe, a terrycloth robe that the hotel supplied, I went out into the living room, and a couple of these cats are already in the room. Cops, plainclothes cops. Then about nine other cops walked in, no uniforms, all plainclothes cops. That's no exaggeration, there were actually *eleven* of these cats." He glanced at Bob. "Right?"

"Correct. It was in the sworn statement."

Buddy lit a cigarette. "It seems so completely outrageous to think about it, even now. So, they come in. And they're just walking around aimlessly. It was a very big suite, the presidential suite. *Aimlessly.* So I said to the sergeant, 'What's happening, what do you want here?' He says, 'We got a search warrant here for narcotics.' I said, 'Oh, yeah? You got a search warrant?' I said, 'Leo, get my glasses.' Got my glasses. So I go to take the warrant, he pulls it back, like so. 'Don't touch it.' All right, okay. So I read it with him holding it. Says they're looking for *heroin.* So I laughed at the cat. And he was—to begin with, he's a real Keystone Kop, y'know? The whole number, he's making a big bust, *The French Connection.* So I said, 'Listen, this is totally ridiculous, man. You won't find any heroin here.' He goes, 'Yeah? We have a search warrant, we'll have a look.' So they start looking. They're all over the place. They're going down the sides of the beds, the pillowcases, lifting up the sheets, lifting up the mattresses, going over the curtains, running the seams of the curtains. One cat went so far—he's looking into the vents of the air conditioners. I mean, it was just unbelievable. I'm standing there, I'm looking at them. Three o'clock in the morning. So I said to the sergeant, I said, 'Listen, while you're tearing the place apart, can I order some breakfast?' He says, 'Yeah.' Real tough cat. So I ordered some scrambled eggs. I'm sitting at the table, eating the scrambled eggs, and there's this cop, a young blond cat, he's sitting next to me, closer than Bob is now, and he's staring at me while I'm trying to eat. While all these other maniacs are running all over the place, he's sitting there, staring at me. Never takes his eyes off me. So, finally, I dropped my fork, I looked at the cat, I said, 'I can't eat these eggs, because you make me puke.' I said, 'If you want the eggs, eat the fuckin' things.' So I moved around, they're all going through their numbers, and one cat runs out of the bedroom yelling, 'I got it, I found it, I got it!' I said, 'What'd you get, man?' He shows the Keystone sergeant, secret-like. Know what he's got? My bottle of sleeping pills. Right? I said to the man, I said, 'If you'd look at the label, it shows my name, the date, and the prescribed dosage.' Oh, no, Keystone won't buy that. He then proceeds to take a capsule out, he breaks it open, he pours some of the powder into his hand, and he does one of *these* numbers!"

He went through a pantomime of the guy sniffing the powder in his hand, dipping his finger into it, cautiously touching the tip of his finger to the tip of his tongue, then smacking his lips. He underplayed the thing superbly and we couldn't help laughing.

Buddy nodded. "You *believe* these guys? So, when he did that—I mean, man, I can't top that. *West Side Story*, right? So, all I could think of, I just said, 'You cats must see a lot of American movies, huh?' They didn't think that was funny. The next cat, he comes out—'What're *these*?' He holds up the bottle like that. So I look. They don't let you touch anything. I said, 'Those are tablets for constipation. They're for your ass. They make you *shit*. No prescription necessary, you can go down to your local apothecary and buy them.' So, next, they're going through our clothes. Like they're looking for twenty million dollars worth of heroin. One cat's an expert on shoes, he tries to slide the heels off, looking for the secret compartment.

"Okay, finally, Keystone asks me who's in the next room. I told him my daughter. He said, 'Your *daughter*?' He thought I had some bitch in there. So he goes, 'Open the door.' I said, 'Don't touch that door, man, I'll open the door.' Okay, I open Cathy's door. She was still sleeping. I don't know how she managed to sleep through all this, but she did. I woke her up. 'What's the matter, Dad?' 'Nothing, the police are here.' 'What's wrong?' 'Nothing.' So, now, Keystone comes in, starts the whole routine again. Sticks his fingers in everything, he even squeezed out the toothpaste. They tore the bed apart, the sheets—it was an unreal experience. It was almost like a movie. They were into the fuckin' tea bag Cathy used to make tea before going to bed. They took a knife and opened the tea bag—a wet, used tea bag. They took a carton of cigarettes, Kents, tore the packs open, even cut into the filters." He paused, stubbed out his cigarette slowly.

"The bathroom thing," Stanley reminded him.

He shook his head. "Oh, yeah, the bathroom thing. In the middle of all this, before they'd gone into Cathy's room, I asked if it was all right to go in the bathroom and brush my teeth. Keystone looks around to see if he gets an okay from everybody. I go to the bathroom door. The door is here." He demonstrated the layout with a glass of water and the salt and pepper shakers. "The john itself is behind the bathroom door and the sink is here. So I'm brushing my teeth, I look in the mirror, and here's this one cat standing right behind me, right on my ass, watching every move. Okay, I brushed my teeth. I didn't piss or anything, I didn't go near the john."

"He wasn't alone in there at all," Stanley adds.

"Right. So then they took Leo downtown, and when they came back again, they had a different search warrant. They'd changed the warrant from heroin, which they couldn't find, of course, to *marijuana*. Now, dig this. They went in the bathroom and just happened to find a little bag of cannabis inside the john. Y'know, inside where the flushing device is? Just happened to be there. They claimed that I'd stashed it there when I went to brush my teeth. They claimed that I'd taken the stuff from my bathrobe pocket and taped it in there. Can you *believe* that mentality? Plus the fact, there was no way for me to get behind the door to the john, because there was a cop on my ass all the time. Well, logic didn't make any fuckin' difference. We were arrested, taken downtown, and booked. We got a lawyer, we put up bail, and we left. We flew to Melbourne and did the concert that night, and it was the best concert we had the whole time we were in Australia. Despite all the bad publicity. It was in all the newspapers."

I waited a while, then: "Well, what happened?"

"Nothing. But the damage had already been done."

"Very bad publicity," Bob said, leaning forward. "What actually happened, by the time it came up for trial, he couldn't be there, but he had a lawyer there. He was found guilty *in absentia* and fined fifty bucks. But from my review of the case, very frankly, I don't think it would've even gotten to an indictment stage here. Because it was a public accommodation, y'know, crowds of people going in and out, it could've been stashed there by any previous guest. In my opinion, I think they tried to flake him. Or maybe he *did* stash it there—who the hell knows?"

Buddy smiled at that. "Fabulous attorney I got, right?" Then he became serious again. "The bad press in this country was one thing, but down *there*—'Buddy Rich arrested on narcotics'—the same size headlines they had in London. But you have to know the press in Australia, man. There was no reason for those stories in the first place, there was absolutely no guilt. I could show you the written statement my lawyer down there presented, with the truth, which they didn't want to hear. I stated, 'I'm hardly a dope smuggler or user. I'm a man going on fifty-seven years of age. I smoke approximately one pack of cigarettes a day. I don't even drink, except for an occasional glass of wine. I've been married to the same lady for twenty-one years. I have a twenty-year-old daughter. I'm not some flunky.'"

I remember being moved by those last few sentences, and by the expression in his eyes.

"Forget it," Bob told him. "What the hell, that was eight years ago."

But he wouldn't forget it, he couldn't seem to let it alone: "The mentality of the Australian police and press has to be experienced to be believed. Their big thing in life is getting blind drunk on beer and then beating the shit out of each other. It wasn't always that way down there, but it is now. Their attitude when they ask you questions. Their arrogance when they talk to you. They get personal, very personal. They insult your playing, they make you feel like an asshole. I figured, from the last time I was down there, which was in nineteen fifty-four, that they were terrific people. They couldn't do enough for you back then. Everything was marvelous. This time, forget it. The first interview—I got off the plane after twenty-eight hours, on the flight from London. Cathy's falling down, man, she can hardly stand up, she's so tired. Here are all these cats out there with their cameras, and we go into the press room, the first thing the cat says to me, he says, 'Don't you think you're kind of old to be playing drums?' That was the first question. I thought he was kidding at first. I didn't think they were actually filming for TV. 'Is it worth your while? Do you make enough money?' I told one cat on the air, he said, 'Do you make enough money to bring your band over here?' I said, 'No, I just came over here because I dig the kangaroos.'"

"It's a simple lack of respect," Stanley said. "Buddy's been touring Australia since he was seven years old, he's no new-comer, they owe him more than that. He was a star over there when he was seven, the second-highest-paid child performer in the world."

Buddy shook his head. "It's not that, Stanley, they don't know that, they don't give a shit about that. It's a lack of respect for jazz musicians. Period. Doesn't make any difference what your name is. If you're a jazz musician, you're a weirdo, a juicer, a doper. That's the image they have of you. Is he a jazz musician?—get a search warrant, tear up his hotel room, he must have something stashed."

"And it's not limited to Australia," Stanley added.

"Of course not." Buddy lit another cigarette, glanced at me. "I don't know how into music you are, but have you ever gone to a classical concert and heard people talking out loud during the performance?"

"No," I said.

"Why don't they?"

"They'd be thrown out."

"Why?"

"For disturbing the majority."

"All right," he said softly. "For disturbing people who enjoy music, who have respect for the music and the musicians. At our new club, we have a rule. Silence during the performances. First time it's ever been attempted in a jazz club, to my knowledge. It works. If somebody insists on talking during a performance, we ask him to leave. In fact, we escort him out. It's only happened a few times since we opened, because I think people know how strongly I feel about it. I want silence when we play. I don't ask for that kind of respect—I demand it."

2

BUDDY'S PLACE WAS then located on the corner of Second Avenue and Sixty-fourth Street, above Sam's restaurant, and the area was ideal for a jazz club, near a variety of movie theaters, restaurants, stores, and specialty shops. The exterior of the three-story building was a clean red brick, recently sandblasted, and the windows were flanked by attractive white louvered shutters. A large vertical sign hanging from the third-floor corner displayed Buddy's logo on top, black lettering on a white drum with sticks, and Sam's logo below, both illuminated by spotlights. The club's entrance was to the right of the restaurant, topped by a small semicircular canopy, and there was a glass showcase next to the door, holding color shots of Buddy in action and giving the times of the shows. Inside, a steep flight of carpeted stairs with mirrored walls led up to a coatroom, closed for the summer, and to the left were the heavy double doors of the club itself.

I arrived about 9:30, the time Buddy suggested. On week nights, the shows began at 10:15 and 12:15, so the room wasn't really crowded yet. It was a relatively intimate room, cool and softly lighted by hundreds of circular white lamps hanging from thin, almost invisible poles, and I could see rows of red-and-white checkered tablecloths fanning out from the bandstand, back to raised banquettes along the walls, and photographs of Buddy in aluminum frames, individually lighted. One of Frank Sinatra's albums was playing quietly and young waitresses moved around tables close to the bandstand, where early arrivals were having dinner. I asked the maitre d' if Buddy or Stanley had arrived; he nodded and escorted me to a table in the back of the room, where Stanley was talking with the headwaiter.

Stanley stood up and shook my hand warmly. "Glad you could make it, Buddy's not here yet, sit down. You had dinner?"

"Yes."

"You want a drink?"

"No, I'm fine, thanks."

"You sure?"

"Yes, really, I'm fine." My eyes were adjusting to the light; I remember glancing around, taking a good look at the place.

"We opened April tenth," he told me. "It seats two hundred and ten comfortably, but we've had close to two hundred and twenty some Saturday nights. Food comes from the restaurant downstairs, same food, same drinks."

"You expect a good crowd tonight?"

"Yeah, Julie tells me we're sold out for the first show. Julie, that's the maitre d'. That's the way it's been since about June, the first show on week nights is booked solid, then it tapers off some, you get the real night people dropping in, you know? But on weekends, forget it, you can't get in here. Friday, Saturday nights, forget it. Like, on Saturday, we have three shows on Saturday. First show starts at eight forty-five. Before the break, there's a line of couples all the way down the stairs and out into the street. Same thing for the third show, goes on at twelve forty-five. Mostly young people, they get out of movies around here anywhere from nine to midnight. Some of them wait on line here close to an hour to get in."

"You must be making money."

He nodded, smiled, picked up a tent card from the table. It read: *Music Charge $5 Per Show.* He glanced around and kept his voice low. "Well, we give people their money's worth, that's the thing, that's why they keep coming back. All right, each person pays a five dollar music charge. So, you figure, an average couple comes in here, say tonight, a Thursday night, not counting the ones that have dinner or a snack, a hamburger. Not counting them. Now, you figure, an average couple will buy maybe a couple of drinks, right? So, we figure, with the music charge, ten dollars for two, each couple will spend a total of about seventeen dollars, minimum, not counting tips. Call it eight dollars each, minimum. Now, take the first show tonight, we're booked. Say, for round numbers, two hundred people. Multiply that by eight dollars. And that's just one show."

"And you work six nights a week?"

"Right, we're closed Sundays."

"Pretty nice piece of change."

"Yeah, well, we got a lot of overhead, don't forget. At the end of the week, when I'm figuring it up, salaries and all, it's not that much. Actually, the way we're going, we need a bigger place."

"Do you personally manage the club?"

"Yeah, I manage, and I'm Buddy's personal manager. I'm here till two, three o'clock in the morning, I close up the place. Then I work on Buddy's other projects during the day."

One thing about Stanley, he was very easy to talk with, right from the beginning. The man was soft-spoken and he looked you in the eye and you had an intuitive feeling that he wasn't trying to con you. I had only met him that afternoon, but I remember that I liked him almost immediately, which is rare for me. His whole attitude seemed to say: "All right, this is me, Stanley Kay. If you like me, fine; if you don't, I'm sorry, but that's the way I am. I don't talk the best English, I didn't have a good education, I'm not young or handsome or rich or famous. But I try to be honest most of the time and I know my business and I work very hard at it."

I knew, through Bob Cavallo, that Stanley had arranged the book project in the first place and that he had a publisher. There was no speculation involved and it gave me a good feeling, because I knew that even if Buddy and I didn't hit it off, which was certainly a realistic possibility, and someone else was eventually signed to write the book, I would leave with the knowledge that I had been dealing with professionals. Which is not always the case in the publishing business. To put it mildly.

From the beginning, Stanley was also a gentle man, and I mean that the way it's written. He went out of his way to be courteous, he really listened when you were talking, he gave you the feeling that he genuinely cared about you. On the other hand, Buddy had come on so strongly at lunch that, in retrospect, it was difficult to believe, much less understand. And that intrigued me. He could have chosen to do just the opposite, knowing that he was about to meet a complete stranger who might possibly spend a great deal of time with him in the future. He could have swallowed the frustration about the taxi driver and come on quietly, cautiously, even eloquently (he can be extremely eloquent, and it's not faked), showing control, even if he didn't feel like it, consciously attempting to make at least an agreeable first impression, as most of us do constantly, wearing the mask of social amenity. But, apparently, he had chosen to come on exactly as he felt—angry as hell. Why? Was that really him at lunch, or was he, too, wearing a mask of sorts, a carefully constructed shell to be used on just such occasions? Complicated people resort to complicated camouflage. I remember thinking at the time that his verbal attacks on the cabbie and the Australian police and press were just too protracted, too strong, too one-dimensional to be anything but defensive. But what was the shell hiding?

Stanley and I continued to talk about the club for a while, and the room started to fill with customers, mostly young people who had arrived early to get good tables for the show.

"How long have you actually known Buddy?" I asked.

Stanley leaned back, looked at the ceiling. "Well, I first became aware of Buddy Rich when my sister and Buddy were child performers at the age of seven and eight, when they were in vaudeville together. And when I started to get interested in playing drums, I was about six or seven years old, and I started to play like most drummers did, on pots and pans and whatever, and just began to follow careers of bands and orchestras. I didn't know anybody, one from the other, actually, until I was about twelve or thirteen years old. And, of course, Benny Goodman was at the height of his career, and that was about nineteen thirty-seven or thirty-eight. And, naturally, there was Gene Krupa, and I watched Gene Krupa, and I remember—"

"Did you live in New York?"

"Yeah, I was born here, on the lower East Side, on East Houston Street. And, just to digress, my background was, I was usually called a street kid, you know, I was always among—a lot of my friends were all hoodlums, rough guys, and a lot of good guys, but I had always wanted to play drums. And my parents watched me and left me alone, they never involved me in any of their problems, or whatever, and they always respected me that I wanted to become a successful drummer. And to go back to your question, I'd remarked to my sister about Gene Krupa, and she says, 'Well,' she says, 'I know somebody that even plays better than that.' And I said, 'Oh, nobody plays better than Gene Krupa.' And she says, 'Well, Stanley,' she says, 'I work with somebody that's a genius.' Who knows, she recognized it then, I guess. And I said, 'Who's that?' And she says, 'Buddy Rich.' So I said, 'Well,' I said, 'I don't think so.' She says, 'Well, I'll tell you what.

He plays at the Hickory House on Sunday afternoon jam sessions with Joe Marsala.'"

"Oh, yes, that was about nineteen thirty-seven?"

Stanley leaned forward, ran his fingers through his thick gray hair. "About thirty-seven, thirty-eight, somewhere in there. And she says, 'I'll call Buddy and tell him you're coming.' And I went to the Hickory House, and it was Joe Marsala's band, and all the musicians used to sit in, and I watched him play. He played a tune, I remember, which was then what we used to call the 'flag-waver,' that was then a fast, fast tune, it was called *Jim Jam Stomp*, and they always had a lot of drummers sit in. And then I remember a few of them sat in that day, and then he came last, and when I saw him play, I said, 'That's the best I've ever seen.' I said, 'I've never seen anybody play like that in my life,' you know, and I agreed with my sister. I said, 'He's the best.'"

"How old was he then?"

"He was about nineteen or twenty."

"Uh-huh. And you were—?"

"Well, let's see, I'm about six years younger than him. I was about—thirteen, fourteen. And then, after that, I began to idolize him, you know how kids do at that age. So when Buddy was still playing at the Hickory House, my sister, Sybil, she got him to come down to our house to hear me play. And I played for him, and I was very nervous, 'cause I remember—and then when I asked her what Buddy said, he said, 'He'll never make it, he can't play.' Yeah, and I remember talking to Buddy about it later on. He said, 'What the hell did I know, I was a kid.' But, you know, that hurt me, I guess. I think I cried, because drums were very important for me to make it, and I wanted him to say I played good, you know?"

I nodded. "But you went ahead anyway."

"I went on and did my thing in music, and joined certain bands later on, 'cause I knew I was good, you know, I knew I could play. And then he finally called me to play in his band. But back then, when we were still kids, I followed him all around. It's an interesting story, when Buddy left the Hickory House, he went with Bunny Berigan, and I followed him around with Bunny Berigan. And at the same time, Artie Shaw was doing a program called *The Old Gold Show*. It was with Robert Benchley. It was CBS, on Forty-fifth Street. CBS Radio played bands then, and you could go upstairs to the mezzanine, and when the door was opened you could look down and you could watch the bands play. And I'd read in *Down Beat* that Artie Shaw's drummer, Cliff Leeman, was going to leave, so he was looking for a new drummer, and I didn't think Artie Shaw knew about Buddy Rich. So, one Sunday, I waited for Shaw after he did his show, and he came out through an alleyway, and I was standing there and I went up to him and said, 'Mr. Shaw, I'm Stanley Kay.' I said, 'I read in the *Down Beat* that you're looking for a drummer.' And I said, 'I know a great one, he's the best of all, Buddy Rich.' And he says, 'Oh, he can't play,' something like that, I remember him saying that, and then next week I read in the paper that Buddy joined Artie Shaw. And I thought that I had gotten him the job, you know, 'cause I was a kid, I didn't know. And then I used to stand on line every Sunday, even in wintertime, and ask people for extra tickets so I could go and watch Buddy play *The Old Gold Show*. And I used to get my ticket and see him, and then I used to run home, 'cause I remember *Ellery Queen* was on Sundays. I used to like to hear the *Ellery Queen* show. That show went on from eight to nine, or nine till ten. I was able to get home to listen to *Ellery Queen*."

He smiled at that, staring fixedly at the tent card on the table. When he didn't say anything for a while, I realized he had become moved by the memory. I listened to the recorded music and tried not to look at him. We heard some voices at the door and he glanced up quickly; I turned around.

"Here's Buddy now," he said, standing. "Be right back."

Groups of young people started leaving their tables and heading for the door, and I could see Buddy there, talking with the maitre d', standing next to the high table that held the reservations book; the table had a small light attached and I could see sharp shadows moving on their faces. Buddy started signing autographs. One of the kids had a camera with a strobe, and I remember a number of flashes that seemed to light up the entire room.

Finally, Buddy made his way to my table. Stanley was with him, and there was another man by his side who looked to be in his early twenties, lean, well-dressed, with thick dark hair and a mustache. The thing that caught my attention first were his eyes: dark, alert to anyone moving close to Buddy. He used his body to maneuver Buddy through the crowd, never actually pushing with his hands, but never stopping his forward motion.

I stood up and shook Buddy's hand.

"Like you to meet Leo Ruocco," he said. "My secretary."

Leo gave me a firm grip and smiled. "Glad to meet you, I've been looking forward to it."

We all sat down, Buddy and Leo on the opposite side of the table, facing the door. People stood around the table, watching, and I remember hands pushing autograph books toward Buddy; Leo stood up and spoke quietly, moving the people back with his body, never pushing. He was about the same age as the kids around the table, and he sure as hell spoke their language, because they were gone within a matter of thirty seconds. When he came back, Buddy asked for a cigarette; it was there in an instant, with a gold lighter. Click, flame, click.

Buddy inhaled deeply, glanced around. "What time is it?"

"Nine fifty-eight," Leo told him.

He nodded, leaned back and looked around, pointed to some-body at a nearby table and exchanged greetings. I remember how completely different he seemed from the early afternoon, as if just coming fully awake. When he smiled in that soft light, he looked very young, and his clothes enhanced the impression—an open-necked yellow shirt with a matching cardigan, trimmed in blue, and the familiar Cardin logo on the upper left side.

"You want a drink?" he asked me.

"You having one?"

"Yeah, I'll have an orange juice."

"Make it two."

Stanley motioned for the headwaiter and gave the order.

A middle-aged couple walked past the table and said hello; Buddy smiled and said something like, "Nice to see you again," then turned his attention to me: "How long you been here?"

"About half an hour."

"What do you think?"

"Nice atmosphere, relaxing."

"We're very proud of the place," he said softly. "Very proud of the way it turned out. It's the first club I've ever had, you know, the first time I've had a home base. I've been on the road all my life. Never had a chance to—you know, breathe a little."

"Must be quite a satisfaction."

"It is." He glanced around again. "I really love the place, you know, I can't tell you. I mean, okay, we have a lot of noise right now. That's cool, that's fine, they can talk as much as they want to before we start playing. Then you get a whole new mood in here, because these people are really into the music. We dim the lights and you can—"

I remember he was looking at the front door then, and whatever or whoever he saw had instantly changed his facial expression. He took a deep breath with his teeth clenched, stubbed out his cigarette and stood up. Leo was up in a flash, also looking at the front door. I turned, but saw nothing unusual.

"Hope you enjoy the show," Buddy told me.

They moved away quickly, Leo leading the way, and entered a door at the back of the room. I turned again and looked toward the front door. Quite a few couples were lined up, waiting to be seated. Julie, the maitre d', was talking with a short, stocky man, who was pointing to something in the reservations book. In the light from that high table, I could see that the man had a bald pate, long and bushy sideburns that swept wide over his cheeks, and an old-fashioned handlebar mustache with long, curved ends, which made him look faintly ridiculous to me. But he seemed to be speaking with some authority.

I turned to Stanley. "What happened?"

"Nothing, that's Buddy's partner."

"The man talking to Julie?"

"Yeah, he owns half the club. Owns the restaurant downstairs."

"They don't get along?"

"No. They don't get along."

The headwaiter brought two tall glasses of orange juice. Stanley took the one intended for Buddy.

"Mel's at it again," the headwaiter told him.

"Yeah, I noticed."

About fifteen minutes later, the club was almost completely filled, and with the front door wide open I could see people packed solidly back to the stairs. The musicians were on the bandstand, tuning up, and the electrician had turned on the basic stage lights, a soft combination of reds and blues. The music stands seemed almost luminous in that light, the same Slingerland custom jobs that Buddy had used most of his years with the big band, and replaced probably dozens of times: a distinctive white marine pearl, matching the frames of his drums, with the familiar *BR* shield against two long vertical stripes.

Around 10:20, I saw Buddy and Leo standing near the back door, and finally Buddy walked toward the bandstand, pausing three or four times to shake hands and speak with people on the aisle. When he took the stage, he went directly to his drums, the houselights dimmed, the stage lights brightened, and—to my surprise, I admit—the entire room fell silent. Buddy gave the verbal downbeat, and they were into *Chameleon*, a reasonably fast opener, that was also the first number on his newest album, *Very Live at Buddy's Place*, released earlier that month on the Groove Merchant label. I had the album at home, and had played it often, but it was exciting to see one of the numbers performed live. That night, it was the same group that had made the album, with one exception—John Bunch had replaced Kenny Barron on piano. Anthony Jackson, the youngest of the group (I think he was about twenty), was on bass; Sonny Fortune, alto and flute; Sal Nistico, tenor; Jack Wilkins, guitar; and Jimmy Maeulen, conga. They looked smart in what appeared to be a brand-new wardrobe, white suits with yellow turtlenecks, and Buddy had changed into a tight-fitting white turtleneck that made him look quite lean as he played. Each time one of the group had a solo, he was hit with a spotlight, and when he finished, there was loud applause. It was a good audience; when the first number ended, they really exploded with applause, whistles and shouts. Then it was *Jumpin' at the Woodside*, one of my favorites, written by Count Basie, followed by the cool mood of *Cardin Blue*, that Buddy wrote himself.

There was a short break, during which Buddy took the microphone, introduced the musicians, and told a few topical jokes in a low-key monologue—throwaway lines that were really very funny—and the crowd seemed to enjoy the poker-faced delivery almost as much as the punch lines. After the electrician set up two additional microphones, Buddy introduced "a dynamite new singing group—three broads we found on the street this after-noon—'Hendricks Getz Rich.'"

They received a good ovation as they made their way to the stage: Michele Hendricks (John Hendrick's daughter), Beverly Getz (Stan Getz's daughter), and Cathy Rich, Buddy's tall, dark-haired, dark-eyed, extremely attractive twenty-year-old daughter. They sang several fast numbers and seemed to blend fairly well together, but I remember it was difficult for me to take my eyes off Cathy. She was anything but a polished performer, yet she had a stage presence and a vivaciousness that was clearly lacking in the others, who were both about her age, and she just seemed to be having one hell of a good time, snapping her fingers, smiling all-out, moving her body to the music, as if dancing in place. I don't know exactly what it was about her, but her whole attitude gave me a happy feeling, and I could see it reflected in the young faces around me. I thought: It's not a job for her, it's not work, it's not a performance—it's a trip.

In honesty, I know very little about the finer points of show business. I see what most audiences see, the obvious. If I remember a particular performance for longer than several weeks, it's an exception. But I recall that night vividly for a number of reasons, and one of them was certainly Cathy Rich. At the risk of overstating the case, there was something magic about the girl when she was on stage: an electricity that you sensed more than saw or heard; an elusive combination of raw talents. What she would do with those talents was not the question for me. That would be a matter for the professionals. For me, it was enough that I had seen her trip. You can't really teach a singer to enjoy work *that* much, and I knew it couldn't be faked effectively at her age. It was unmistakable, and it was exciting, and it was also sad, in a way, because the vehicle for that kind of trip is delicate beyond belief.

After "Hendricks Getz Rich," Buddy and the band played for another half hour or so, and finished with a rock chart called *Giggles*, in which Buddy tangled delightfully with Anthony Jackson on bass. They played around and against each other, carrying on a definite "conversation" with their instruments— soft, loud, sweet, sour, laughing, crying, loving, fighting—and finally it was time for Buddy's solo. There had been bursts of laughter and staccato applause during *Giggles*, but then, when the crowd somehow sensed it was time, the atmosphere in that room changed drastically. I remember the hush, and the way people leaned forward in their chairs, and the strong feeling of expectation: This was what they came to see. It was always the same when Buddy played.

I leave it to the musicologists and professional jazz writers to continue their determined attempts at describing a solo by Buddy Rich. I have studied literally hundreds of these well-intentioned, convoluted, technical descriptions, I know them by heart, but I simply decided to withdraw from such scholarly pursuits. I don't believe anyone can adequately describe any given solo by Buddy Rich. No writer I have ever read has come close to the essence of the solo, for predictable reasons, and, in my opinion, it is a serious error of professional judgment to try. I may be wrong, but it seems obvious to me that a solo by Rich is so much more than the sum of its parts, that any attempt at a clinical analysis is an exercise in music myopia. You have to experience the total phenomenon—technique, dexterity, speed, virtuosity, emotion— to catch even a glimpse of what it's all about. He's telling you something about himself in every solo, each one is different, and what he's saying just cannot be translated into words. The man feels music so intensely that when you actually see him, hear him, react to him, you know instinctively that it's primitive emotion, not intellect. But more than that, you know that he's on a trip. It's always a trip, a world of his own, where the distinctions between illusion and reality are not always clear to him, and where it is often very lonely.

That night, when the solo ended, there was the split-second hesitation, and then it came, all at once, deafening. It came in the dark with only the spotlight on him, as he made his way to the microphone, dripping wet, using a towel to wipe his face, and it got louder. Louder when half the room stood up and shouted; louder when the houselights came on, changing the mood, illusion to reality, cigarette smoke hanging; louder than ever when he was up there, up at the microphone, blinking, the forehead wet, standing straight, listening to it, accustomed to it, feeling the vibrations, poker-faced, waiting, gauging the right moment, finally pointing with the towel to each musician as he introduced them, but you couldn't hear the names. Anthony Jackson was last, and there was a roar that lasted longer than the others, and then Buddy motioned for them to sit, a slight wave of the towel, nothing extravagant, and it was over. The voices stopped, then the applause, then the chairs were banging as they sat, then silence. It was like that when Buddy played.

3

THE NEXT WEEK had been proclaimed "Drug Prevention Week" in New York, and on Thursday afternoon, July 18, I went with Buddy, Stanley and Leo to a drug prevention music clinic for youngsters, located in a building on Amsterdam Avenue at 159th Street, up in the Washington Heights section in Manhattan. It was one of many run-down, overpopulated neighborhoods in that area, with a predictably high crime rate, where drugs of almost any kind were sold on the street to anyone who had the price. During the summer months, drug action was particularly heavy, with all the kids out of school, no work available, few recreational facilities, and virtually nothing to do. When we arrived about two o'clock, the stoops of the tenements were jammed with kids, garbage cans overflowing at the curbs, and a fire hydrant had been opened just up the street, giving a few kids at least some relief from the heat.

We were met at the club by Sylvia Cutts, the director of the program, a small, gentle woman, apparently almost blind. She shook Buddy's hand, then moved her face close to his. "Mr. Rich, there are no reporters present, and if any show up, we'll take you to a private room."

As Stanley explained later, that was one of the stipulations: No publicity of any kind. Whenever Buddy performed for youngsters (which was fairly often, as I saw for myself), the press was excluded, and there were no exceptions to the rule. It wasn't any big deal, he just felt strongly about that kind of thing.

Leo parked the car on the opposite side of the street, as Buddy, Stanley and I followed Mrs. Cutts into the building, which looked like it had been a school at one time. There was a hand-printed sign at the entrance: "District 6 Drug Prevention Program. A Music Workshop. 2005 Amsterdam Avenue. 3rd Floor. Welcome All." We were given a one-page agenda at the door.

Upstairs, the kids were separated into four small groups in different rooms: saxophone and flute; drums, guitar, bass. Our room was about thirty feet square, with about 100 folding chairs, half of which were occupied. I think the group was all boys at that point, ranging in age from around six to twenty-five. It was very warm. Everyone was sweating. A large, noisy fan was blowing warm air toward the open windows in the back. Leo came in and set up a single snare drum on a tripod.

When Mrs. Cutts introduced Buddy to the group, he was sitting on a high stool behind the drum, wearing a New York Yankees baseball cap (given to him by pal Sparky Lyle the night before at the club), jeans, and unlaced sneakers. At first, it was difficult to hear Mrs. Cutts, because someone was playing a saxophone in the next room. Stanley went in there and asked the guy to cool it for a few minutes, but when the sax stopped, it was still hard to hear because of the fan.

Buddy nodded to the applause, then asked Leo to turn off the fan. He began by giving a demonstration of how to hold the sticks, and when he started playing, it sounded quite loud in the small room. Within seconds, kids were hurrying into the room and fighting for seats, and he had to stop the demonstration and wait for everybody to settle down. When he continued, every chair was taken and kids were standing against the walls and sitting on the floor in front. I counted eleven girls in the audience.

After about half an hour, Buddy started a rap session by asking for questions. That was actually the most important ingredient of the clinic: not to entertain a passive audience, or to lecture on the dangers of drugs (which would have been the worst possible approach for this particular group), but to hear *their* ideas, to stop and really *listen* to them for a change, and, most importantly, to give them straight answers. Straight answers about what they could do if they really wanted to get into music. Not what they *should* do, but what they *could* actually do, if they were serious about it and wanted it badly enough and were willing to work at it.

I remember the majority of them were teenagers and, judging by their questions and the way they asked them, you knew damn well they weren't about to be conned. Buddy understood the fact.

The first question came from a teenage girl who hadn't been there for Buddy's introduction. She was slumped down in her chair with her feet in the aisle, chewing gum and cracking it.

"What group you play with?" she asked.

"Various bands, doesn't really matter."

"Yeah, but what group you play with *now*?"

"The Buddy Rich band."

She nodded, cracked her gum. "Never heard of him. Who's Buddy Rich?"

The room broke up with laughter.

Buddy played it poker-faced. "He's the bandleader. He couldn't be here. I'm just the drummer from his band."

The kids really enjoyed that; it was their kind of humor and they had a good sense of it, laughing all-out, even applauding. One very young boy in the front row shouted: *"You're* Buddy Rich!" He received a loud ovation.

"Hey, how's Johnny Carson?" somebody yelled.

"He's better," Buddy said seriously. "Last I heard, he had his brain returned successfully."

It went on like that for a while and it was intriguing to see how the mood began to shift, ever so gradually, to some serious discussions: problems faced by Gene Krupa; reasons for the second bass drum; importance of finding a good teacher; pretentiousness of electronic amplification of drums; necessity of being able to "read" music today. One of the most intense youngsters talked at some length about Carl Palmer, the young British drummer who had five platinum records to his credit and was already a millionaire at twenty-four. Was it true that Buddy had given him his first lessons in London when he was a teenager? Buddy told the story, briefly, of how Carl had come to his hotel, asked for advice, received lessons, and how they had eventually become close friends. He placed stress on the fact that Carl had succeeded because he wanted it so badly that he absolutely refused to quit, regardless of the obstacles. He told the story low-key—the plain, simple truth. Toward the end of the session, the very young boys started asking questions that they had probably been waiting to ask from the beginning:

"You got a Rolls-Royce?"

"No."

"Why not?"

"Don't need one."

"What kind of car you got?"

"Mercedes."

"Mercedes. Mercedes-*Benz*?"

"Yes."

"Are you a millionaire?"

"No. Not even close."

An older guy: "Well, you own your own club, don't you?"

"Own part of it."

"How much your full drum set cost?"

"About a thousand dollars."

A boy in his twenties: "Yeah? I know about a drummer who paid six thousand dollars for his drums."

"Yeah?" Buddy answered softly. "I know a cat who paid thirty-five thousand dollars for his drums."

"Thirty-five *thousand*!"

"Yeah. But the thing is, it doesn't matter how much you pay for your drums. The only thing that really counts is how good you can *play* them. Right?"

Of all the things Buddy said all afternoon, that was the only one that drew silence. Just a few seconds, and I remember looking at the young faces, black, white, brown, glancing at him, all sweating in the heat of the room, maybe thinking about that statement.

Then, finally, an older voice from the back: "You still maintain that you're the best?"

"I never said that. I merely say that I can play with the best drummers in the world and hold my own."

"How long you been playing drums?" the voice asked.

"About fifty years."

"How old are you?"

"Fifty-six." Then, almost defiantly: "*Five six*."

"Could you turn on the fan?" a girl asked.

"Could I? Yes!" He motioned to Leo, then broke into a circus-like drum roll, increasing in speed and volume, climaxed by a very loud *bang*, as Leo simultaneously snapped on the fan.

They ate it up, laughing and applauding, and then Buddy was into his solo, giving it the full treatment, start to finish, dripping with sweat, off on a trip somewhere. It must have lasted at least ten minutes, and I will never forget the faces of the kids, their eyes, which was the most moving experience of the afternoon for me, and Stanley's reflective expression, leaning against the door, watching them.

After a tremendous ovation, he stayed around for a while, his T-shirt soaked through, letting some try to play the drum, answering questions for others. I remember one little boy, who couldn't have been more than six, if that, came up shyly and asked to play. He wore a sailor's hat, a brand-new Snoopy T-shirt, and red trousers. Buddy got behind him, held his hands on the sticks, and guided them through a fast number. It was one of those times when I really regretted not bringing along a camera. You should've seen the kid's face.

Outside, Buddy was swamped by autograph seekers in front of the building, then again across the street, where they surrounded his car. We were parked in front of a small store, and a kid in his twenties stood in the doorway and shouted: "Who's the big *star*, man, who's the big star giving *autographs*?"

He kept yelling the same thing, over and over, and I saw Buddy glance at him several times. He was a husky black guy and I don't know if he was drunk or stoned, but suddenly he went straight for Buddy, shoving the kids aside, shouting at the top of his lungs: *"Who's the big fuckin' star giving autographs!"* Leo was out of the driver's seat fast, sprinting around the car, but it was over before he got there. Buddy waited until the guy was almost on top of him, then spun sideways and unleashed a karate kick to the groin. The man went down. It happened so fast and there was so much confusion that I could only get a glimpse of the man on the sidewalk, over on his side, legs moving, holding his crotch. Then he was up quickly, shouting at Buddy, but moving away, still bent over. Challenge withdrawn. Buddy continued to sign autographs.

Back in the car heading downtown, we talked about it, and about the clinic and the kids.

"Drug Prevention Week?" Buddy said. "Why not Drug Prevention *Year*? Why not Drug Prevention *Decade*?"

His dressing room at the club was relatively large and comfortable, on the top-floor corner, and that night you could see long lines of headlights, five lanes wide, moving south on Second Avenue, and hear horns and the steady hissing of tires on warm asphalt. Large color posters of Bruce Lee dominated the white walls, and the furniture was black against a red carpet. There was a large-screen television set and a completely stocked bar for his guests, of which there were many between shows when a variety of musicians and celebrities would drop in.

About 10:30, Buddy went down to play the first set. Leo and Stanley went down with him and I was alone with Marie, his wife, for the first time. I had talked with her earlier in the week, first at the club and later at their apartment, but never at any length. I remember Marie so clearly that night, sitting back on the big couch, almost dwarfed by it, drinking a cup of tea: a slim, fragile, strikingly attractive blonde, with the face of a girl in her twenties and the hands of a middle-aged woman, wearing a chic denim outfit. Her voice was soft, often musical, sometimes fragile, occasionally hard, and there was a breathless quality in her laugh, like Cathy's laugh, completely uninhibited. We talked about Buddy for a while, then I shifted the conversation to her.

"Were either of your parents in show business?"

"No," she said. Then: "Well, my mother worked in films before she married. My dad was going to Stanford, studying to be a doctor."

"How did *you* get started in films?"

"Well, I don't know, I was kind of pushed into it, because all my life my mother, jokingly, would say to me—" She hesitated, took a sip of tea. "She had been under contract to Max Sennett, and they decided to pull her out of the Max Sennett bathing beauty line and star her, so they began giving her the star treatment. And there was a clause in her contract that said she couldn't be married, but she had secretly eloped with my dad. And when they started to give her all this stuff, she was like three or four months pregnant with me. And that was the end of *her* career."

"That was right in her contract, that she had to stay single?"

"Oh, yeah. And she used to say, 'Okay, I didn't make it because of you, so now *you* do it.' And being out there, and going to school out there, and being exposed to it, you know, Hollywood and all my friends and everything…"

We heard the band break into their first number, directly below us. Marie stood up, went to the corner window and stared down at the traffic. She was silent for a few minutes, listening to the music, then turned toward me slightly, leaning against the wall, arms folded, still looking at the street. I remember half her face was lighted by the "Buddy's Place" sign outside on the corner of the building. She looked small and lonely.

"Well, I went to USC first." She continued to look at the street. "And I married a boy from USC. His father was the Los Angeles city treasurer, and he was an All-American football player, Mickey McCardle. We were married about a year and a half, and it was during the war, and he was in the Marine Corps, after USC. We were married in Quantico, Virginia, we had a military wedding. He went to Officers Candidate School in Quantico. And then I came back, and he was stationed in Quantico, and I came back to Los Angeles and stayed with my in-laws, and decided that I wanted to go to work, rather than go back to school. My mother wanted me to go back to school, but there was no need at that time. So I started working in films. I went on an interview and I was chosen and the first film I worked in was *George White's Scandals* at RKO."

"How many films did you actually make?"

"God, I don't know. I mostly studied at RKO. I was at Metro, but I was under contract to do *The Pirate*, with Judy Garland and Gene Kelly. And that's—they would just use the kids, they'd use the contract players, and just throw them into the pictures. And, in the meantime, you got to study, you got your drama lessons free, and you had your money coming in. But you did whatever they told you to do, you did background. So I did some musicals at Metro and I did a couple of things at Twentieth and I made a test at Twentieth and nothing happened with it. I never did bother to see it. I had a very bad experience with the contract player that tested with me. He looked exactly like Clark Gable. And he was very, very upset, because it was keeping him from being a big star. So we're doing a love scene and he's whispering to me and I'm saying, 'Darling, I adore you, I love you,' and all this stuff. And in *this* ear he's whispering, 'You no-talent bastard, you'll probably become a star.' And I didn't have enough drive to go and say, 'This man is doing this to me.' I was just—you know, I'm terribly insecure, and I had to marry someone like Buddy, who's very strong and powerful and overpowering."

"But you had a fairly long film career, didn't you?"

She shook her head slowly, negatively.

"I thought I read somewhere—"

"No, it wasn't," she said flatly. "I never had that—it sounds like I'm copping out, but I never had that drive that it takes to become a star. I really always just wanted to marry somebody that could take care of me, you know, some man that I could love and would take care of me nicely. That was really the career that I wanted for myself. So I was working in pictures because I was kind of pushed into it, because of my mother, and it paid better than anything else, and it was glamorous. But to have that drive—when it came right down to the bottom line, John, where, okay, you can have the part if you go to bed with me—oh, and I was under personal contract to Howard Hughes, too."

"You were?"

She nodded and seemed to brighten with the memory. "Howard is really weird. He was the wealthiest man I ever dated, and also the most eccentric. You know, you've heard all the stories about Howard Hughes. And he adored me because he couldn't quite figure me out."

"Why? What'd you do?"

"I guess everybody else was just terribly nice to him for what they could get out of him, you know? And I would make dates with him, and I'd stand him up. He was also one of the oldest men that I dated at that time. And, okay, so he was wealthy, but kind of weird, and if I got a date to go out with some young guy, I'd go out with him, and I wouldn't have enough courage to call Howard and break the date, knowing full well that he'd try to talk me into it, so I'd just avoid that and stand him up."

"How did he react to it?"

She smiled, glanced at me. "He wanted what he couldn't have; he was like that. Anyhow, he used to do all of these tests of me, and we'd go and look at them, and he'd say that I had trouble with my sibilance. You know, my *s*'s, which didn't come across really good, and so I was going to a speech class to learn how to work on my sibilance. And he was paying for my drama lessons, and I was getting a couple of hundred dollars a week, and I had a Chevrolet to drive that belonged to Hughes Tool, because every year they bought a whole fleet of Chevrolets. And it was okay. And I'd have dinner with Howard every once in a while. Now, my apartment was in Hollywood, and he had an estate in Bel-Air. So, if we went to Mocombo, for example, coming home from there, you'd turn left on Sunset Boulevard to go to my apartment, and right to go to Bel-Air. And he'd always start to turn toward

Bel-Air, and I'd grab the wheel and turn it back. So I guess he got a little tired of that. So one night we're pulling out of some club, and he starts to turn toward Bel-Air again, and I said, 'No, Howard, I really want you to take me home.' So he reached in his pocket and pulled out a pair of drop diamond earrings."

I had to laugh, visualizing it, and she laughed too.

She held her thumb and forefinger about three inches apart. "I swear to God, they were this *long*! And he held—he took them out of the jewel case, and he held them up, and all the cars are going along Sunset Boulevard, and the headlights were hitting these diamonds—it was fantastic. And I said, 'Look, not even for the diamonds.' And he says, 'Okay, Marie,' and he puts them back in his pocket. I mean, I wanted to study and I wanted to be a star— if it came easily. But when it came right down to going to bed with somebody, I just wouldn't do it that way, I became very insulted. There were a lot of people who made it that way. I went to bed with who *I* wanted to go to bed with. I'm not telling you I was a Virgin Mary, either, it's just that I didn't want to do it that way. If I had been attracted to Howard, then it wouldn't have been a problem. I just liked him very much, period. Another thing, he'd always call my mother when I stood him up. My mother was married twice, and my stepfather's name was Brazil. Howard had a real block, he couldn't seem to remember that name, so he'd call and say, like, 'Hello, Mrs. Madrid?' And she'd laugh hysterically, she'd say, 'Howard, did she stand you up *again*?' Then he asked my mother and I to dinner one night, and he took us to Ciro's. It was on the Sunset Strip, and right behind it was Sunset Plaza Drive, where all the stars lived in all these great homes. Well, after dinner, he pulled the car up Sunset Plaza Drive, and I said, 'Howard, where're you taking us?' He says, 'There's something I want to show you.' So we wound around, around and around, and we went right up to the top on Mulholland Drive, which is the top of the mountain, and the view up there is fantastic. And we pulled into this little house, overlooking the entire city of Hollywood. It had a swimming pool, a sauna room, zebra-skin furniture, fur rugs—just unbelievable. And he had the deed to the house in his pocket, and he says, 'This is yours.' And he said to my mother, he says, '*But*, you've got to move in here with her.' And he says, 'I want her to have this house.' And I said, 'No.' Because I knew he was going to lock me up, because he did that later with several other girls he went with for a while. So I kept saying no, and finally it just—nothing happened with it. The contract ran out and was never picked up."

She went to the coffee table, took a sip of tea, then sat on the floor, leaning against the couch. "But I always liked Howard. I genuinely liked him. I thought of him as a very good friend."

"Did you see him much after that?"

"The next time I saw Howard was after Buddy and I were married."

I sat on the floor, cross-legged, next to her. I remember being surprised at how easily she talked, as if she had long since decided that we were on the same wavelength.

"It was in Vegas, when Buddy was playing there, we were with Harry James and Betty Grable." She paused, glanced at the ceiling; her blue eyes were transparent in that light. "We were at the Flamingo Hotel, and somebody had a hot roll going, and the gambling table was just filled with people, because this guy was throwing all his numbers, and everybody was betting with him, and it was very lively. And all of a sudden, I looked up." She demonstrated with her hands: "Betty and Harry were standing here, and Buddy and I. I looked up and I felt—you know how you can feel somebody staring at you? I looked up, and there's Howard, across the table from me, and he gives me this shy little smile, and I waved to him. And before I knew it, he'd worked his way around all these people, and he's standing right next to me over here—here's Buddy and here's Howard—and he leans over to me and he says, 'Tell me, is he as good in the feathers as he is on the drums?'"

4

CHICAGO WAS HOT and humid on Friday evening, August 9, 1974, streets teeming with people, newspapers carrying banner headlines about Gerald Ford, who had been sworn in at noon that day as thirty-eighth President of the United States, following the resignation of Richard Nixon. I checked into the Ambassador Hotel, then walked along crowded State Parkway. People were in particularly high spirits, smiling, laughing, shouting, even singing, and with good reason. The depressing political events of the past several months were finally over, like a nightmare, and you could feel the vibrations of relief, of people looking forward to happier times, as if the changing of a president would somehow solve most of our problems. It may seem naive in retrospect, but I remember the feeling was contagious, a mood of euphoria, compounded by the heat and glitter of night and the weekend. I headed toward Mr. Kelly's, the supper club where Buddy and the band were playing a two-week engagement. On the way, one of Chicago's largest record stores had a lighted marquee, no less than forty feet long, reading: "Downtown Records State Parkway Salutes Buddy Rich at Mr. Kelly's." It was on the opposite side of the street, and I stopped and stared at it, then crossed over to see the elaborate window display of his new album. The store was open and crowded, as were many other stores along the way.

Mr. Kelly's was on North Rush Street at East Bellevue Place, and the whole area was alive with people wandering around the outdoor exhibits of the Gold Coast Art Fair. There was a kind of carnival atmosphere, with streets blocked off to traffic, and thousands of paintings, sculptures, and art objects of every description lining the sidewalks. North Rush Street was jammed with clubs and bars—Alfie's, Jazz Showcase, Bourbon Street, Faces, Pat Haran's, The Backroom, Jay's, Larry's—but the big modern facade of Mr. Kelly's seemed to dominate at a glance, and the brightly lighted marquee had bold capital letters announcing: BUDDY RICH AND SIX.

I had arrived about 9:45, just as the first show was ending. In the lobby, I talked with Jerry Dambra, the club's general manager, who had been expecting me; he took me inside and it was so crowded that I had to stand halfway up the stairs to the dressing rooms. The band was playing *Billy's Bounce*, and I noticed two changes: Joe Romano had replaced Sonny Fortune on alto sax, and Angel Allende was now on the conga drums, replacing Jimmy Maeulen. When the number ended, the applause was loud and long from a capacity audience of just over 300, mostly young couples, and Buddy made his way to the microphone. He looked lean in a white silk shirt embossed with delicate, scattered patterns of deer, and he was tanned from several weeks in California; the band had played the closing concert of the Concord Summer Festival just the previous weekend.

The room was finally quiet and he had just started to thank the audience when we heard two voices at the front door shouting, *"Buddy!"* Everybody turned, and when they saw Woody Herman and Gerry Mulligan walking in, a chain-reaction of noise and confusion started—hundreds standing to see, dozens rushing over to get autographs, flashbulbs going off all over the place. Woody and Gerry maneuvered toward the stage, shouting and waving at

Buddy, and it was very obvious that neither of them was feeling any pain. They jumped on stage, shook hands with Buddy, threw their arms around him, hugged him, and the ovation was tremendous. Gerry grabbed Sal Nistico's sax, Woody got a clarinet from Joe Romano, and after a brief, hilarious tune-up, they launched into a jam session that was hot, spontaneous, and genuinely exciting to watch. I have no idea how long they played, and I can't even remember *what* they played, but every number broke up the house to the extent that all 300-plus people stood up and shouted, *"More!—More!—More!"* in a rhythmic chant, until the musicians, dripping with sweat, had almost no alternative but to continue. Finally, Woody and Gerry simply ran off the stage and tried to get out, but they were immediately surrounded. It was wild for a few minutes, then cooled down, and people returned to their seats.

Buddy took the microphone and called out, "Woody, where you playing?"

The crowd hushed somewhat, but there was no answer. It was dark in the audience, of course, and in all the movement and confusion, I wasn't even sure that Woody and Gerry were still in the room.

"Woody!" Buddy called. "If you're standing, blink!"

There was laughter, and then some guy in back shouted: "Rich, *he* held *you* up!"

In the pause, I remember Buddy standing rigid in the spotlight, unable to see the man, and by his face and posture alone, without a word, you knew that he was enraged, as he always was with hecklers. I was surprised at how quickly the silence came, in a room of that size, almost from his first sentence, the easy way he said it, his face dripping in the spotlight: "Stand up, man, let's see what you look like."

He paused, just momentarily, and nobody stood up or moved, and with the pause everything changed. It changed with the jut of his chin and his eyes widening and the forward lean of his posture; it changed with his voice—loud, sharp, fast in one sentence, then so quiet, gentle, hesitant in the next that you had to lean forward to catch the words. "You must be from Boise, Idaho, man. The big swinger from Boise, in the big city for his once-a-year big night on the big jazz scene. Stand up, man, stand up, so everybody can see what a real jazz critic from Boise looks like."

He lit a cigarette, inhaled deeply, waited. Smoke curled up and flashed through the long shaft of light.

Then: "You know what you are, man? You're a *coward*. That's right. You're a coward. You're a coward from Boise, Idaho, who gets his kicks by sitting back in a dark room and yelling insults at artists. That's right—*artists*. Musicians who've worked very, very hard for many years to get to the top of their profession, just like everybody else does. Musicians, artists, who're busting their asses up here to entertain you. And, believe me, it's God damn hard work, no matter how easy it looks to somebody with your mentality. I call you a coward, right out in the open, right to your face, which I can't see because you don't have the guts to stand up and act like a man. You hear me?"

Then another pause, longer, Buddy blinking, starting to form words, hesitating, lips working. And the crowd waiting.

Then, softly: "If you're a man, stand up right now, and I'll walk outside with you, quietly, and we'll go someplace where we can have complete privacy. Just you and me, one-on-one. If you're not a man, continue to hide in the dark. Because you need it."

Nobody in the room moved. Nobody said a word.

Finally, Buddy spoke in a tired voice. "Ladies and gentlemen, I apologize to you for the unpleasantness. It's just I've been fighting guys like that all my life, and I guess it's too late to stop now. You've been a marvelous audience all the way and I thank you for that. People like you make it all seem—to cats like Woody and Gerry and me—like it wasn't all in vain, all the years."

I remember the heavy silence when he left the microphone and disappeared from the spotlight, as if nobody knew quite what to do, and then, as he stepped off the stage, the room just seemed to ignite with a long, loud, shouting, standing ovation, which lasted—and even intensified—as he walked all the way around the room to the stairs, and all the way up to his dressing room. I followed him up and he ushered me inside.

He slammed the door and leaned against it. "That son of a *bitch*!"

"He doesn't matter," I said quietly.

"He *does* matter! One guy like that can spoil the whole evening, all the fun."

The dressing room was actually two rooms, and he walked slowly to the one in the rear, taking off his shirt, which was soaked through. The areas were fairly large, with black imitation leather furniture and thick carpets. Buddy sat at the dressing table in the corner, looking very tired. Leo came in quickly, nodded to me, and went back to help him change. Within a few minutes, Woody and Gerry came in, laughing and singing, followed by Don Osborne, a tall, heavyset man, who was president of Slingerland Drums, and his son, Don Jr., who looked to be about twenty or twenty-one.

Leo served cocktails to them, and we sat around and talked, and the way Woody and Gerry were carrying on, Buddy couldn't help but cheer up. I remember Woody was wearing a handsome khaki-colored safari outfit and drinking vodka on-the-rocks, having a hell of a good time, probably celebrating the day's events in Washington. I knew he was sixty-one that year, but I had never seen him close-up, and his age was hard to believe, especially with the good tan. Gerry, in a denim jacket and jeans, was forty-seven then, but with his long blond-gray hair and beard he looked much younger. I noticed that he wasn't drinking anything, and he sure didn't need anything.

After ten minutes or so, there was a knock on the door. Leo answered it, and Bobbi Arnstein came in smiling, Hugh Hefner's executive secretary, whose far-flung responsibilities included the Playboy Mansion, Hefner's home in Chicago, where Buddy was a regular guest whenever he was in town. I had heard a lot of praise about Bobbi, who was then one of the few women in the hierarchy of the Playboy empire, and I wondered how I'd react to her. There was a sense of cool confidence in the way she shook hands, looking steadily at you and no one else, and her eyes had life and humor, behind slightly oversized glasses. Her high forehead and finely chiseled features were framed by thick blonde hair that tangled at the shoulders of an exquisitely tailored pastel-blue pantsuit. She was thirty-four, and she looked and acted thirty-four, which was refreshing.

Buddy had known her for years, she was one of his favorite people, and when it was time for the second show he asked me to take good care of her, which I did with pleasure. We sat at a table in the back, on a platform that gave an excellent view of the bandstand, had several drinks, and talked during the break between the second and third shows.

Afterward, we followed the crowd out into the warm night and waited for Buddy in front. It was almost three o'clock, but the area was still relatively active, particularly the blocked-off streets around us, where hundreds of people moved among the colorful exhibits in the Gold Coast Art Fair, and you could still sense a mood of celebration. Bobbi and I had a cigarette and watched everything and the warm air was very pleasant, and smelled good, after hours of air conditioning. Also, it seemed quiet and peaceful, following all that music. I remember admiring her necklace, which looked to me like a string of some kind of animal's teeth, but she explained that they were eagle's claws, a gift from a friend.

Before long, Buddy appeared at the door with Leo, and after signing a few autographs, he suggested that we walk back to the mansion, rather than ride, because it was such a beautiful night. Bobbi took his arm and they walked in front of Leo and me.

I think that was the first time I had a chance to really talk with Leo for any extended period, because he was always so busy with Buddy. He was a good-looking guy, in his early twenties then, but he came across a lot older, with a calm, collected attitude and voice, and his dark mustache helped the older impression. He seemed really alive and animated at three in the morning, like Buddy, as if he had just caught his second wind, because they always slept into the early afternoon. I recall how alert his dark eyes were as we walked through the art exhibits, taking everything in, especially the girls.

Leo told me about his early years, born in the Bronx, but raised in Yonkers, where he went to school. He dropped out of high school when he was sixteen, did virtually nothing for about a year, and became severely depressed. "I finally got out of that," he told me, "I went to a psychiatrist. I was really down and out, I was ready to jump. And I came to the conclusion that there's nothing in life worth getting up-tight over. I learned a lot from that experience. When I was about twenty, I started to get gigs playing drums."

"Joined the union, the whole thing?"

"Oh, yeah, I joined the union, went through that whole thing, played all those rotten wedding gigs and everything. And I was working in Massachusetts with a trio, and I heard that Buddy Rich needed a band boy."

We were on State Parkway then, with scattered couples and groups walking leisurely, shadows doubled and tripled on the sidewalk by lighted store windows, bright streetlights, and head-lights moving past, and I remember how Leo glanced ahead quickly, as if suddenly realizing that Buddy and Bobbi were with us. They weren't, actually, they had become separated from us by about thirty yards then, with maybe a dozen people in-between.

Still, Leo lowered his voice. "So I heard that Buddy Rich needed a band boy. Now, he was my idol. You know, I didn't listen to anyone other than him whenever he was on a show, I had his instruction books, I used to dream about studying with him, because he was the greatest drummer in the world. And, you know, for years and years I had that on my mind, I really wanted to be a drummer and I really wanted to make something of myself, but I didn't have the facilities and know-how to go about doing it."

"Had you seen him in person?"

"Yeah, several times I'd seen him in person. I was very impressed with him. Very impressed. But there was something I resented about him. I don't know if it was a jealousy that I knew I'd never play as well as he did, no matter how hard I tried. And there's something, I think, that every drummer has when he sees Buddy play. For some reason, there's just some arrogance or some-thing that comes out, and there's a resentment, knowing that you'll never be that good. And he kind of—sticks the knife in there. When someone tells him, 'Oh, that was great,' he seems to say, 'Well, I know,' although he never says it,"

"I know what you mean."

"I can't actually put my finger on it, but I know that there was—even though I loved him and respected his drumming, there was some resentment in there that I could never really figure out, even up until today." He took a deep breath. "Anyway, I heard that he needed a band boy, and I called the manager and I said, 'Yeah, I'd really like to take this job; I'm working now as a musician and I'd drop that and everything.' And he said, 'Okay, come on over to the hotel,' and I went over—"

"Who was his manager then?"

"Bill Miller. And I went to the job where Buddy was playing, and I listened to the band. And I couldn't believe it, you know, Buddy Rich, man, like he's my idol, and I have a chance to work with him. So I met Buddy. The manager said, 'Come on in and meet Buddy,' and I went in and I was, you know, like *this.*" He made his hands shake, then came up with an excellent imitation of Buddy's voice: "He says, 'This the new band boy?' I says, 'Yes, sir.' He says, 'Well, you know, you have a hard job, you have to take care of my drums and make sure everything is in order, you have a lot of equipment and everything—can you *handle* it?' And he made—I might have said the wrong thing and he snapped at me. So I said, 'Yeah, sure, I'd love to have the job.' And he says, 'Okay, you got it.'"

"Just like that?"

"Yeah. And I'd never lifted a suitcase, I'd never really had any job like that, but I kind of—faked it, you know, I said. 'Yeah, I'll do it.' And I took the job and I did nothing but concentrate on the job. I mean, I did everything I could possibly do to get it right. For some reason, I really wanted it to work, because I wanted to work for him."

"You started almost immediately?"

"Yeah. I started immediately. Setting up the instruments, and I knew nothing about it, and I really wanted to get it right."

"This is where, again?"

"This is in Boston. He was playing at—a place they closed down, it belonged to—I can't think of it now. It was a place that Buddy loved, he played in Boston many times. The band always stays at the Bradford Hotel in Boston. So I went on the bus, and I worked for a month, I carried the bags, and I carried his bags, and went out to get him sandwiches at night. And, you know, I tried to be very nice. If I did something wrong, I'd take the abuse of being hollered at, or if the drums weren't right, or if something was wrong, I'd say, 'I'll get it right,' and I'd *do* it, you know, life or death. If Buddy wanted something, I'd tell the guy, '*We have to have this.*' And I spent every second of the day being very forceful with people, sometimes, just to get everything right, the way Buddy wanted it. If he'd say, 'Want this, this, this, and this, and if it was totally impossible, I'd say, 'Yes,' and I would *do* it, I would *find* a way to do it. And to this day I never say, 'No,' to Buddy. Anything he wants, he has, and I put everything I have into doing it, and I think that's why he digs me. So, after a while, he said to me—see I was just taking the band boy's place for a couple of months, because he'd wanted to go home and—"

"This is the big band?"

"This is the big band, yeah."

"How many members?"

"Approximately sixteen or seventeen. It was a hard job. I had like fifty pieces to handle, you know, on the bus, one-nighters and everything. But I did it, man, there was a satisfaction and I enjoyed it. Then, when the band boy came back, Buddy said to me, 'You travel with me, you come with me. And you take care of my clothes and take care of my appointments and my minor business.' So I started driving with him in the car, and I'd read the map and get directions, and do all little things like that. And we'd stay up nights and talk about different things and we got to know each other fairly well."

"Did he call you a secretary at that time?"

"Well, for the longest time we didn't know what to call me. Whether to call me valet or secretary, and finally we decided, okay, I'm a secretary. That would be the best title for me."

We were approaching the Downtown Records store, with the salute to Buddy on the enormous marquee, which was still lighted. Leo pointed to the marquee and we both stood there and laughed, it was so big. The store was closed, but the windows were still lighted, so we stopped and looked at the album displays, including Buddy's.

"So, actually," I said, "you were the band boy just a couple of months."

"Just a couple of months, until the regular guy came back."

"This is about nineteen seventy-one?"

"No, this is seventy-two. And then, like, when the vacations came, I went everyplace Buddy went, and I ate with him, and, you know, did everything he did. We went swimming, we had vacations, I went to his house and he put me in his guesthouse."

"Where is this?"

"In Palm Springs."

"Oh, yes, he had a home there."

"Yes. And I got to be friends with Marie and Cathy and they all liked me. And we did things together, we went to the movies and this and that."

"So you were sort of a member of the family."

"Yeah. Oh, yeah, very much a member of the family. I mean, there wasn't a detail that went by that I wasn't exposed to. Whether it be a personal thing in the family, whether there was an argument or something, I was a member of the family and I would just sit there. There was nothing hidden from me. Buddy has never hid anything from me, whether it be from the most personal things in his life to business. If Buddy had an appointment with a celebrity or something, even though I was a little raggedy, 'This is my brother, this is my friend, this is Leo.' He took me with him. And I loved him for that, because he was, you know—he *is*—a friend, an honest friend."

We continued walking. Buddy and Bobbi were out of sight by then, but we really didn't want to keep up with them.

"Do you regret the fact that you didn't continue as a drummer?"

He hesitated. "No, because I'm constantly learning from Buddy. Just from watching him and listening to him. I'm satisfied with that. I still play a little bit, but—I really don't know if I want to be a drummer any more."

"Why?"

He thought about it. "I don't know. I think because I know that I'll never be as—great as Buddy is. And it would frustrate me."

"But you're in a position to learn things that no other young drummer in the *world* would be able to learn."

"Right."

"Every single day."

"Well, you can only learn from Buddy just by watching him, because Buddy's not a teacher."

"Yes, but isn't that the best—?"

"He plays all those great things, but he can't really explain it, technically, because he hasn't developed it, it just came to him very easy."

"Suppose you left him, would you go on to be a drummer?"

"That's the only thing I could do, I guess."

"Would you want to?"

"Would I want to? I think so, yeah."

"Do you have a strong desire to be a drummer?"

"Yeah, I think that would be about the only thing I could do."

"Where do you see yourself going? You're satisfied now, obviously."

"Yeah, I'm satisfied now, yeah."

"Are you projecting into the future?"

"No, unfortunately, I'm not. And I can't. I really can't, because I'm working for Buddy, and if I project into the future—I mean, I think of things I'd like to do, but I know that unless I put the effort into it, they would never even be possible."

"What about money? Are you satisfied with what you're making?"

"Well, what Buddy's giving me? Buddy's a very generous man."

"Okay."

"But Buddy gives me more than just a regular salary. I mean, I live just as well as he does, and he lives elegantly. I eat just as well as he does, and he gives me all the clothes that I have, and he's like a father to me, you know?"

"Do you think, for example, being so close to the guy like this, that a girl would fall short? That she just wouldn't come up to this kind of—for openers—companionship?"

"No, but what I do think is, I don't think I can be close with Buddy and close with a girl, too. There's no room for a woman, you know, and that's where I feel deprived, in that area, because I can only have a one-night relationship with a girl. We're traveling so much, and it can't go any more than that. And I really don't know how to manipulate to make that one-nighter thing work."

"Suppose something happened and you left Buddy? After being that close to a human being, do you think any girl could live up to that?"

"It would have to be in a different way, a totally different way."

"There would certainly be a void."

"Yeah."

"Because very few people get that close to anybody."

"Right."

"You'd have a vacuum to fill, which would be very difficult to fill."

"Very. The only thing I miss now—I have everything with Buddy, some days are good, some days are bad, but I'm very happy with him. The only thing that's missing in my life is love from a woman. And I don't mind a one-nighter. Like, all the girls that I've gone out with, even though it may be for only one night, I really *love* them. For some reason, people think that you can only love one person. Like, when you get married, 'until death do us part,' and all that jazz. I mean, why do people think—how can you put down on paper that you're only going to love one person for the rest of your life? What's wrong with loving a man and a woman, or two or three? I mean, if you have a lot of love to give, and you give it honestly, how can you be expected to confine all your love for just one person?"

5

Noon the next day, I went to the Playboy Mansion, 1340 State Street, which was just a short walk from my hotel. It was a warm, lazy Saturday, with the smell of freshly cut grass from well-watered lawns, and the trees along the street were bright green in the early August sun, casting dark patterns on the narrow sidewalks and the tops of parked cars. When I reached the mansion, I crossed the road to take a good long look at it. On a street of sedate old Gold Coast mansions, the exterior didn't seem to stand out in any respect but size, primarily length, because it was actually two connected buildings, 1336 and 1340, identical in architecture, and the latter was the original structure. Both were four stories of red and gray brick, tall windows and balcony doors framed in white stone, and the steep slate roof held ornate garret windows and multiple chimneys. A black wrought-iron fence enclosed the manicured shubbery and lawn, and I remember the second-floor windows were like enormous green mirrors, reflecting the crowns of the trees.

The original building had been constructed in 1903 for Dr. George Isham; when he died in 1926, his family leased it to a contractor who divided it into apartments. In the early 1940s, it was purchased by a parking lot tycoon named Robert Lydy, who began extensive restorations. Playboy bought it in 1959 for $400,000. When I first saw it in 1974, its value was estimated at triple that amount. The mansion had a total number of seventy-four full rooms, with facilities for thirty-eight permanent residents in separate apartments and dormitories, and girls employed as "Bunnies" in the Chicago Playboy Club were permitted to live there at a nominal rent.

There were seven special guest rooms frequented by Hugh Hefner's personal friends, including Bill Cosby, Tony Curtis, Vic Damone, Sammy Davis Jr., Jessie Jackson, Elia Kazan, Hugh O'Brien, George Plimpton, Buddy Rich, and Mort Sahl. Although Hefner spent most of his time at the then-new Playboy Mansion West, in Los Angeles, the Chicago mansion still had regular house functions, such as Sunday feature films, various business meetings of *Playboy* magazine's editorial staff and board of directors, luncheons, dinners, benefits, and parties.

Two smartly dressed men were standing in the shade of the white stone pillars at the front entrance. I introduced myself, and one of them escorted me into the vestibule, where he dialed Buddy's room on the housephone and announced me. The man then took me inside. Everything seemed dark because my eyes took a while to adjust. We turned left in the hall and passed through two rooms, then climbed several flights of stairs. The man stopped in front of a heavy wooden door with the inscription "Leather Room"; he knocked, waited until Buddy answered, then left.

"Did I wake you up?" I asked.

Buddy smiled, waved me in, closed the door. "It's okay, it's cool." His voice had gravel. "What time is it?"

"Quarter past twelve."

"You had breakfast?"

"Just coffee."

"Sit down, grab a magazine, be right with you."

He went into the bathroom and in a few seconds I could hear his electric shaver under the soft stereo music. The big high-ceilinged room had a pronounced black-leather decor—chairs, couch, tables, lamps, even the base of the very low, square, king-sized bed, which looked like he'd just jumped out of it. Recent copies of *Playboy* and *Oui* were on the fitted carpet near the stereo console, his New York Yankees baseball cap rested on the black marble of the fireplace, and there were newspapers stacked on top of the television set. I went over and picked up a copy of that morning's *Chicago Sun-Times*, which was opened to an article about him with a large photo. He looked good in his glasses and he was gesturing with his hands. It was an article by Neil Tesser, and I particularly enjoyed the ending, when Buddy stopped sparring with the guy and got down to cases. It began with a quote from Buddy that made me smile.

"The whole idea of my club is to present the best music—not small—or big-band, not jazz, not labeled anything but first-class entertainment. The only two forms of music in any field are good and bad. What happens in-between is up to the taste of Middle America, which has no taste at all, whether it be in politics or music."

Buddy says his place has gotten a reputation as a "no rip-off" club, but stresses that the musicians come first, the audience second.

"We tolerate no foolishness from drunks, from anyone. If you cannot behave, you cannot stay. In the four months we've been open, we've thrown four people out, because they were abusive— not to the artist, but to the room.

"In my place, if you don't like what's going on, we'll pick up your tab and say, 'Get out!' We don't have any bouncers or any fuzz—just me and two other guys."

Actually, just Buddy is probably enough. After 11 years of study, he has earned a black belt first degree in karate which, he says, he never uses except in practice and competition. And there's plenty of time for practice, since he refuses to play the drums except on the job:

"I never practiced drumming; never had a set of drums, sticks or practice pad in my house.

I play when I go to work. I make as many mistakes on the job as anybody could possibly make. But I think it's better to do it there than to sit down and have to work something out and then have it be a mechanical thing."

No one ever accused Buddy Rich of false modesty, but he says that charges of conceit and egotism have been false accusations.

"It's not an ego thing with me. I'm the most confident man, for what I do, on earth. And I say whatever I say because I can back it up. If that's misconstrued as ego, it's on the listener's part.

"I'm accused of being super-arrogant. I'm not. I'm just super-sure of myself. I'm very positive about my own talent. If I make a statement, I can back it up. Like the theory in karate. A guy doesn't walk into a bar and say, 'I'm gonna beat up everybody in the house.' What he does say is, 'I'll take half the house.'"

Positively.

Buddy came out of the bathroom looking far more awake than when he went in. He picked up the telephone on the bedside table, pressed one of the lighted buttons, and spoke softly to someone, saying that we were on our way down to have breakfast.

He slipped on some clothes and we went downstairs, walked along a lengthy oak-paneled hallway, our footsteps echoing, and finally paused at the top of a short flight of steps leading to one of the most enormous and lavishly furnished living rooms I had ever seen. Actually, as Buddy explained, it was called the "Ballroom," which is essentially what it had been under its original owner, just after the turn of the century. We stood silently for a moment. No one was in the room. Long, thin shafts of sunlight slanted from the high windows to touch exquisite leather couches, luxurious armchairs, statues, paintings, glass tables holding *objets d'art* that reflected the sunshafts like prisms. As we descended the steps, guarded at floor-level by two knights in full-plate sixteenth-century armor, I remember how Buddy told me some fact about the room in a quiet voice:

"The room is fifty feet by thirty-five feet. Looks a lot bigger, but that's it. Whole thing was originally constructed in England for some cat, then dismantled and shipped over in numbered pieces. Walls are paneled in solid oak. Floor is inlaid teak. Fireplace is marble, made in Italy." He glanced up at the very high, beamed ceiling. "Ceiling was hand-carved and hand-decorated, also imported piece by piece from Italy to England, then here."

I walked over to see the painting above the huge fireplace. It was Picasso's famed *Femme Nue Endormie*. To the left, in the southwest corner, was a kinetic sculpture titled *Domino Machine*, by Gordon Barlow. Behind the white couch near the fireplace was a long, narrow table holding a glass-topped stereo complex that was easily fifteen feet long. Buddy walked to the north wall, which had a black-and-white painting, *Mister*, by Franz Kline, and a painting that I recognized at a glance, Alfred Leslie's *Playboy of the Western World*. I went over to take a closer look, and as I did, Buddy pressed a switch that rolled back a huge section of the wall to reveal a projection room with two thirty-five millimeter movie projectors covered by clear plastic. He laughed softly, closed the section of wall, and I walked across the room to see the "screen wall," which also had a built-in television screen to the right, and over that, an intriguing wall sculpture, *Virgin*, by Frank Gallo, the same artist who did the beautiful sculpture, *Woman Walking*, by the couch. The painting near the piano attracted my attention,

Wednesday, by Jack Tworkov, and as I was studying it, Buddy laughed again.

"Come on, let's have some breakfast," he said quietly. "Before you have a shit hemorrhage."

I nodded, glanced around. "I've never seen anything like this, anywhere."

"Nobody else has, either."

"You guys tend to take stuff like this for granted."

He shook his head. "Nobody takes stuff like this for granted."

The breakfast room was around the corner from the "screen wall," and had about six or eight tables, all empty. We sat by the painting *Yardgoods*, by David Hickman; almost immediately, a young white-jacketed waiter came out and took our orders. Buddy lit a cigarette.

"So, where're all the Bunnies?" I asked him, smiling.

"Don't believe everything you read, John."

"I thought they'd be all over the place."

"Bare-ass, like in all the pictures."

"Absolutely."

He inhaled deeply. "Well, if you want it straight, I told them to cool it, to stay out of sight while you were around."

"Decent of you."

"Didn't want you to have indigestion."

"Really thoughtful."

"Told 'em that cats like you don't take it for granted."

"Nobody takes stuff like that for granted."

"Actually, they're pretty much restricted around this part of the house," he said seriously. "Like, they're invited to the Sunday movies and some of the special functions, the parties, but that's about it. Bobbi restricts them to the dormitory area, you know, the connecting house, and they like it that way. They work hard at the club and they want privacy around here."

I remember a vague feeling of disappointment when he said that, and then, almost instantly, I felt angry at myself—or, rather, at my subconscious—for actually entertaining some idiotic fantasy that the mansion would somehow be peopled with beautiful young girls just hanging around, talking with famous actors, musicians, writers, directors, whatever, like the party pictures in *Playboy*, all dedicated to the enjoyment of "the good life." It was a childlike fantasy, buried so deeply in the subconscious that it was obliterated at almost the instant it surfaced—a simple twinge of disappointment—but it had surfaced, unmistakably, and that surprised me.

About halfway through breakfast, still a little annoyed at myself, I heard footsteps and looked up to see two absolutely stunning girls walk in; without any exaggeration, they could've stepped right out of the pages of *Playboy*. They had dark tans, long hair, wore very short white terrycloth robes, and seemed surprised—even embarrassed—to find guests in the room, like schoolgirls caught breaking the rules.

Buddy took it in stride. "Good morning, ladies, good afternoon—whatever."

"Hello, Mr. Rich," the taller one said; the other one said, "Hi," and smiled at us. They turned and padded barefoot to a table at the far end of the room.

Buddy laughed silently, watching me, then leaned forward. "Don't look now, man, but you just drooled egg all down the front of your shirt."

Afterward, we went up to his room, played records and talked, and when Leo arrived we decided to go down to the pool. We wore only short terrycloth robes, identical to those worn by the two girls, and apparently *de rigueur* around the mansion. On the way, Buddy showed us the famed sculpture, *Girl on Saddle*, by Frank Gallo, just inside Hefner's private quarters. Walking along the hallway toward the Ballroom, he pressed a certain spot in the paneled wall, and an entire section of the wall slid back silently, revealing a white-carpeted spiral staircase leading to one of the guest suites. Leo and I had to laugh out loud at that one. It was just too much.

At the northwest corner of the Ballroom, near the stereo library (which had literally thousands of albums), we went down a narrow flight of stairs, through a heavy door, and emerged in the pool area, which I can only describe as mind-blowing. From air conditioning, you stepped into a pleasantly warm, distinctly South Seas atmosphere, complete with coral formations, exotic and fragrant plants and small trees, giant Polynesian statues, and a free-form swimming pool, forty feet long, with a cavelike opening at water level, leading to a hidden "grotto"; the water was kept at a constant temperature of seventy-two degrees. Buddy pointed out an underwater window at the deep end of the pool, and explained that it was part of a lower-level bar, where you could watch the swimmers.

There was an adjoining sauna room, sunlamp room, game room, gymnasium, even a bowling alley. We went into the game room first, a plush and thickly carpeted L-shaped area, with a handsome pool table in the center, flanked by a total of eighteen game machines—predominantly new electronic video games of eye-hand coordination, shooting, driving, tennis, hockey, space missiles moving through patterns of meteorites—everything you'd expect in a modern amusement arcade. There were tables with copies of *Playboy* and *Oui*, big bowls of fresh peanuts and cashews, cigarettes of every brand, and Hugh Hefner's personal matchbooks, which were in almost every room in the mansion.

Buddy picked up a little booklet that listed the stereo selections by number, dialed several numbers on a gadget that looked like a touch-tone telephone dial, and we had soft jazz to play by. We each picked out a machine, played it, then moved on to the next, sometimes playing each other. You pushed a red button next to the coin slots, and every game was free. It seems funny now, but I remember feeling exhilarated, rushing from one machine to another, like a kid let loose in an amusement park where every game is free, and the fantasy thing returned again—triggered, I suppose, by having seen the pool area—a fleeting subconscious question, strictly rhetorical, asked to make an asseveration and not to elicit a reply, asked by the little boy inside me, laughing with the pure joy of a new mystery: Is it all true, after all, can people really live in a chocolate factory?

When we went back to the pool, Leo decided to go in the sauna room, and Buddy took me to a storage closet near the deep end that held dozens and dozens of brand-new swimsuits arranged in drawers marked by size, men's to the left, women's to the right, trunks and bikinis of every shape and color. The closet also had an assortment of snorkel tubes and masks, flippers, and several complete sets of scuba-diving gear. We selected swim trunks, left our robes on the chairs against the wall, and Buddy removed his small hairpiece before diving in. It was the first time I'd seen him without it, and I must admit it surprised me. The water was really pleasant. We swam quietly for a while, listening to soft music from stereo speakers around the pool, the jazz selections Buddy had dialed in the game room. Naturally, I swam into the cavelike "grotto" and had a long look around. The area was lighted in shafts of delicate reds and blues, a private little pool surrounded by wide stone ledges with brightly colored plastic mats. I went up and sat on the top ledge, and it was virtually impossible not to conjure up visions of wild, uninhibited parties past, even if they never took place. It almost had the feel of a real cave, except for the music from another stereo speaker in the high, hidden ceiling.

Outside, Buddy was standing in the shallow end, leaning against the edge.

"Find any Bunnies in there?"

I swam over to him. "Absolutely loaded with them."

"I was going to come in and rescue you, but..."

"Man, I fought like a tiger."

"Just too many of 'em, right?"

"Like a zoo. I tried to scream, but..."

"Too many tits in your face, I know."

"I thought they'd never let me go."

"Actually, I signaled them to cool it, I felt sorry for you."

"Just in time, too, they were starting to bite."

He laughed softly, narrowed his eyes at the water. "Funny, every time I go swimming, which isn't that often, but every time I do, I remember my time in the service, in the Marines. I joined in nineteen forty-two, because I wanted to fight, I wanted to get right in the action, you know, couldn't wait. We were coming back— we'd been out for about ten days on LST, making landings on the beach outside of San Diego. That whole area then belonged to the Marine Corps, they had something like thirty thousand acres. Camp Pendleton was the largest Marine base in the world at the time. That whole area from San Diego up to—I suppose up to LaJolla, was all Marine Corps."

"It was an enormous area," I said.

"Oh, it was ridiculous. And, you know, the cliffs and every-thing are hanging over there, so we'd come in and make these landings, simulated landings, and we'd get an air cover to come in, to soften it up. But the more I got into it, the sillier it got. Here we were, grown men, taught to yell at a fictional enemy. You were supposed to imagine deadly Japanese, which I found to be hysterical. And these gung-ho Marines were really going at this beach like they were going right into Guadalcanal. We came up the beach, we came up about a hundred yards off the water. It was raining like a bastard. And we were to dig in. The air cover had softened it up. We were going to come up all the way into the training area, we were just going to storm it."

He turned, lifted himself up the edge of the pool, then sat there for a moment, blinking, staring at the water.

"And what happened?" I asked.

He made his quick, nervous cough, continued to stare at the water. "So, I'm digging and digging and digging, and I was tired and I was filthy and I was wet. You can't imagine how dirty you can get until you've worn the same boots and socks, and the same fatigues, for five or six days without taking a bath or anything. I took my trench shovel off my pack, and I was digging, and the next thing I know, I heard, 'Dig faster, you Jew bastard,' and I got a kick in my ass, and I went headlong into the hole. And that's all. All I know is, I had this trench knife—it's a knife and a shovel—in my hand, and I fell. I let go of the thing and I came up. I didn't know who it was, all I saw was a face in front of me, and I just really zonked it, and this cat went down. And it wasn't twenty seconds when I had two forty-fives right smack in my face, with the hammers back. Two MPs, one on either side. This guy gets up and says something to the effect, 'You won't be out for a long time.' I said, 'Fuck you, motherfuck,' or whatever was hip in those days. And they ran me up in a Jeep, put me in the back with hand-cuffs, and got me back. And I'll never forget the CO, he was the only other Jew besides me in the whole fuckin' base."

The way he said it made me laugh, and I remember the sound echoing slightly, and then Buddy laughed himself.

"Yeah," he said, blinking again. "It was hysterical to me because—you think back to about nineteen forty-two and the great amount of anti-Semitism that was around. We had the Nazi thing in Jersey, real heavy Jew-haters over there. And my first eight weeks out of the first ten weeks of boot camp, it was 'Jew this' and 'Jew that,' and fights all over the place, and I was ready to fight the war here, rather than fight it over there, because I could feel that much hate over the fact of being Jewish. Anyway, I was brought up to face a summary court-martial."

"Which is what, actually? I never understood the difference between a summary court-martial and a general—"

"A summary court-martial is not like a general court-martial, where you can go to jail for up to ten, twelve years, whatever they give you. This thing is just for minor offenses against military law. In a summary court-martial, it's just your CO and two lieutenants, and they listen to you, the various reports of what took place. So, the articles read that at no time should you discuss politics or religion in the service, because you have too many opposing factions."

"That's right, I remember now."

"You know that, right? The guys in my group told the CO what happened. He kicked me, hit me, and he called me a Jew bastard. They immediately shipped him out. He was a major. I got thirty days restricted to barracks, while they waited for a cell to do eleven days on bread and water, which they call 'ten and one.' You do ten days and on the eleventh day you get out. Then, for thirty days I did garbage details. Now, the garbage detail, I'd sit in back of the truck and they'd throw all this shit at you, and when you finally got up to the dump, you were up to here in garbage. I did that. I also swept down theaters, broom bullshit, I did that, and then, when that was over, into the barracks and no getting out for thirty days. Finally, on the thirtieth day, they came and got me, we went back to the CO, I was given a physical. And a strange and funny thing, they took me to the stockade, and as I was having my hair cut—because they shave your head, man, they get another brig rat, that's what they call prisoners in the Marine Corps, 'brig rats,' and they got another brig rat to shave my head bald—as this was happening, Susan Heyward was coming out. She'd been there to visit one of the officers or something. And I knew her from Brooklyn, she's from Church Street in Brooklyn. And this cat is going up the middle of my head, and she looked down at me, like, 'I know you from some place.' And it was just a quick 'Hello,' because I wasn't allowed to talk, 'cause I was under arrest. She asked why I was there, and there was no answer to her. Okay, next, they take me to my cell. You have to see—you have to be there, the cell is six by six, so they make sure you have no place to walk, and if you're six-foot-two, you're out of luck."

"Six by six by six?"

"Yeah, six wide, six long, and six high. Now, the cell itself has nothing. Concrete floor and wood stockade like the old-fashioned forts, rolled lumber, and the door had a slit." He held his fingers apart. "Three inches, four inches—that big—and that was the *only* light. And I had a choice. They threw a blanket in, and you could either cover yourself and sleep on the concrete floor, or put the blanket on the concrete floor and not have anything to cover yourself with. And it would get cold like a motherfucker. And the only—they gave you some fatigues with a great big stenciled 'P' in yellow on the back of the jacket, which makes a good target if you try to run out, because if they hit it with a light, it glows. Now, they had a catwalk that used to go around the entire circle where the solitary cells were. And at first I thought, 'I can handle this, I can just set my head to it, I can handle it, a little whistling, a little humming.' The minute you go—" he whistled softly—"there's a cat at the door-slit, screaming, 'Knock it off, brig rat!'"

"It's a wonder you didn't go nuts in there."

He nodded. "I know some guys who came very, very close."

Leo came out of the sauna room, walked to the closet at the deep end to get swim trunks, then made a smooth, deep dive. You could see his body in the lighted water, distorted by waves, coming up slowly. Buddy watched the ripples move toward us; the light flickered on his face. His eyes seemed almost hypnotized.

"Then they would do things like this to harass you," he said, so softly that I had to move closer to hear. "I used to put the blanket up against the wall, and sit on half of it, and cover half of myself. And they would come in three times a day, the only time you knew what time of day it was. They'd come in early in the morning and they'd bring you a loaf of bread, and you could break off as much of the bread as you wanted. And then another cat was there with a pitcher and these white porcelain cups, and he'd pour a cup of water. Now, the rules state that they're supposed to give you salt, so that you can swallow the dough. There's something about putting salt on the bread, so that when you mix it with the water it's not quite as..." He paused, frowning, watching the ripples lap at his legs.

"Not quite as hard to get down," I said.

"Yeah. Well, they didn't do that. They didn't give me any salt. The first couple of days, you walk around and you feel like you've got a fuckin' Pinto inside your chest. That lump, that white dough, when you drink water, it makes it hard, it doesn't go down, it stays right there. So then you learn how to do it. You eat the crust, the outside of the bread, drink a little water first. But these are all things you learn. So, you'd know that three times a day you'd get that. And on those occasions you would also be taken out, with two MPs, and they would walk you to a large 'john,' and you would brush your teeth with your finger, because you were not allowed to have a toothbrush or anything else, and do whatever you had to do, but you had only a few minutes to do it. Then, about face, and right back in." He shook his head slowly, remembering, and dropped the subject. After a while, Buddy and I went into the sauna room, which was relatively small, and sat on the lower half of what seemed like a teakwood bunk bed. The steam was warm and pleasant, and we were relaxed and sweating nicely, when he started talking about the prison again, as if he just couldn't push the visions from his mind.

"I had guys who particularly hated me in there, because I was a New York wise guy, although I had never seen any of these motherfucks in my life. But your record comes down with you and it says, 'New York' and 'musician.' So I would get things like this: I would try to get to sleep, and all of a sudden, a sergeant would bust in and have his right hand on his forty-five. 'Get up, brig rat!' You stand at attention. Fuckin' time—it could be four in the morning, it could be four in the afternoon. He'd say, 'You got cigarettes in here?' 'No, sir.' I think the hardest part was saying 'sir' to these little assholes. 'No, sir.' Okay, he'd call another guy in and this cat's got a bayonet. He goes around the walls, poking his bayonet between the logs, and he comes over and says, 'What's this?' And it'd be a cigarette butt."

For just an instant, my mind flashed back to Australia.

Buddy sat forward, staring at the shower wall directly ahead. It was difficult to see him clearly, with all the steam, but I remember sweat pouring down his face, and the fixed stare, and the inflection of the voice, as if he were reliving the incident, and the pain.

"It'd be a cigarette butt," he said, louder this time. "Says, 'Where'd you get that?' 'It's not mine.' 'It's not *what*?' 'It's not mine, sir.' 'Step outside.' Went outside, hands straight down. They're walking you, there'll be four or five guys—this happened to me several times, it's not just once—they'd say, 'All right, where'd you get the cigarettes?' Over and over again. For guys they don't like, they do all of these numbers. 'Where'd you get the cigarettes?' 'Those are not my cigarettes, sir.' 'They're not *your* cigarettes? Where'd you *get* them?' And I used to go, 'Look, you know what I'm wearing.' 'Stand at *attention*, boy, nobody told you to talk!' 'All I'm asking—' '*Shut up!* How long can you stand on one foot, boy?' 'I don't know.' 'Let's try it. And let's try it at *attention!*' When you stand that way for what would seem hours, now you begin to realize, by trial and error, that you have only two answers, and both of them are wrong. They say to you, 'Are you tired, boy?' 'Yes, sir.' Says, 'Let's try it on the other foot.' So you just reverse it, standing at strict attention. These guys are playing poker, or whatever they're playing, and they ignore you, and you just start to fall. There's no way you can stand, and when you start to fall, they shout, '*Get your foot up there, boy!*' 'I can't stand it any more.' 'You can't *what?*' 'I can't stand it any more, sir.' 'Oh, you *can't?* Well, try the *other* one now!' They make you do it for half an hour, back and forth, and then they ask you again, 'Are you tired, boy?' So then I said, '*No, sir!*' Says, 'Well, *good*, just stand that way for *another* half hour!' And the pain gets to you, and you start to fall. '*Get your foot up there, boy!*' And you know there's nothing you can—"

"Don't think about it, Buddy. Come on, let's grab a shower and—"

"And I got out," he said softly. "I came out of there—and you can verify this with my brother, Mickey, next time you see him—and I weighed something like a hundred twenty-five, a hundred twenty-eight pounds. And my mother took one look at me, with this uniform hanging off me, and the eleven-day beard, and my hair just starting to grow out a little bit, and, at first, she didn't even recognize me. And I got a three-day pass. They took me back to L.A. And when you've gone that long without eating, you can't eat. Your stomach shrinks. My family, they were giving me all this beautiful food, and I couldn't eat. But I swore that when I got out, there wouldn't be one day in my life—"

He turned quickly, glanced at me through the steam, then frowned, as if suddenly aware of my presence. I don't think I'd ever been in a sauna room before, and I remember the whole atmosphere seemed unreal to me for some reason, almost halluci-natory, a fragment from a dream. But the last thing he said, before we left the room, remains frozen in my mind, probably because of the intensity in his voice:

"I swore that there wouldn't be one day in my life, *ever*, when I would do anything for any branch of the armed forces—except for the *kids*, who are doing the actual *fighting*."

Toward evening, after a good workout in the spacious gym, we took another shower, went up to the Ballroom, and watched television for a while. A waiter came out to take our dinner orders, but Buddy wasn't hungry; he went up to his room to rest, because he had three shows to work that night at Mr. Kelly's.

Leo and I dined alone, in the same room where Buddy and I had breakfast, and we were very relaxed in just our terrycloth robes. We both had the easiest thing possible, steak and salad, because we didn't want to cause unnecessary work for the chef, and we had a bottle of red wine, St. Julian, '69, which was superb. Before coffee, Leo excused himself and went up to Buddy's room to change. I lingered over coffee and had a couple of cigarettes.

When I walked through the Ballroom, on the way back to Buddy's room, the long August daylight had finally softened, and my attention was drawn to a small red light up on the landing near the entrance to the hallway. As I walked toward it, I was surprised to see Bobbi Arnstein standing there in the semidark-ness, next to the source of the red light: a little glass case on a pedestal containing the delicate statuette of a glass horse. Bobbi glanced up when she heard me, and her face and hair were bathed in the light.

"Haven't seen you all day," she said, adjusting her glasses.

"We've been down at the pool."

"Where're Buddy and Leo?"

"Went up to change." I glanced at the statuette in the glass case.
Her voice softened. "Lovely, isn't it?"

"Yes. It's a strange light."

"The horse is a holographic projection."

"A holographic—?"

"Projection, yes. *China Horse*, by Gordon Barlow."

I nodded, looked at it closely. Holograms were still rare in
those days.

"Haven't seen one before?"

"No."

"It's a three-dimensional image stored on a high-resolution
photographic plate, exposed with a laser. When you develop the
film and light it with another laser, it re-creates the image in space."

I leaned down and studied every detail of the horse. It looked
absolutely solid, like any other statuette. The thought crossed my
mind that she was putting me on, and I had to smile.

"I know," she said. "It's hard to believe at first."

"Bobbi, are you telling me—that thing isn't there?"

"That's right."

I maneuvered around all four sides of the case, my face right
next to the glass, then I looked at it from the top. "It can't be an
optical illusion, it's too *solid*."

"If you removed the glass case—but don't do it—and tried to
touch the horse, you'd see. If I turned off the holographic
projector and snapped on the room lights, you'd see. It's the most
accurate three-dimensional illusion of reality ever discovered.
The man who developed the theory of holography received the
Nobel Prize for Physics in nineteen seventy-one. Professor Dennis
Gabor of England."

I took a deep breath and studied it again. Despite what she said,
it was difficult to suspend belief in what my eyes were seeing,
clearly, right before me, as a solid object.

Bobbi reached around the pedestal, pressed a switch, and the red light in the glass case vanished instantly, leaving us in semi-darkness. I heard her footsteps moving away from me, down the bare wood floor of the hallway, then a click, and the overhead lights blazed on. I blinked in the sudden brightness and looked at the glass case. The little horse was gone. In its place was a smoky glass with gray-green swirls. As so often happens when your senses deceive you, I found myself laughing softly. I walked around the four sides of the case again, inspecting every inch. The little horse had disappeared—or, rather, it had never been there as a solid reality.

"I'll be a son of a bitch," I said.

She turned off the room lights, came back, reached down on the pedestal, and switched on the holographic projector. The little red horse flashed to life, solid as ever. Bobbi was on the opposite side then, crouched down, and I watched her through the glass. I remember the way she pushed back her long, tawny hair, and adjusted her glasses by pushing her finger on the nosepiece. Her eyes seemed like a little girl's.

"This is my favorite art object in the house," she told me, almost confidentially. "I turn it on every once in a while just for fun, just to remind..." She paused, wet her lips.

"What, Bobbi?"

"Oh...just to remind myself of something."

"Of what?"

"Oh, it's just..." She straightened up, glanced away.

"What is it, Bobbi?"

"Maybe I'll tell you later, when I'm in a better mood."

"Okay."

She looked in my eyes, almost as if she was afraid she had hurt my feelings. "Is that okay?"

"Certainly."

"I'm starved, I'm going to have dinner. Have you eaten?"

"Just finished."

"Okay, see you later."

She smiled warmly, turned and walked toward the Ballroom, and I took one last look at the little red horse, then went up to join Buddy and Leo. But I didn't see Bobbi that night, or the next day before I left for New York, or, as it turned out, was I ever to see her again.

Just five months later, on the night of January 12, 1975, the thirty-four-year-old Bobbi Arnstein left the mansion with only a small purse in hand, walked five blocks to the Maryland Hotel, registered under an assumed name, chained and bolted the door to her seventeenth-floor room, and carefully swallowed lethal doses of barbiturates, sleeping pills, and tranquilizers, bringing her sensitive life to an end.

6

TORONTO WAS OVERCAST and humid when I arrived on August 17, with showers predicted and the chance of a thunderstorm. I checked into the Seaway Towers on Lake Shore Boulevard, where Buddy was supposed to stay, but he hadn't registered yet. Stanley and his wife, Sandi, had checked into room 1221, but when I called from the lobby there was no answer. I was given a room near theirs, on the top floor, and my terrace faced south over the long green stretch of Marine Park and Lake Ontario. The water was deep blue and I could see many sailboats in the distance. After unpacking, I called Stanley again, without success, then sat out on the terrace, relaxed, had a cigarette, and read *The Toronto Star*. The front page carried an orange-colored banner headline, "Swimmer Cindy Wins Metro's Heart," and had two large photographs of Cindy Nicholas, the sixteen-year-old who had just broken a twenty-year-old record by swimming Lake Ontario in fifteen hours and fifteen minutes, lopping a phenomenal six hours off the previous record.

I turned to the entertainment section, where there was another banner headline, "Lawrence Welk (gasp!) Planning to Jazz It Up," and half the page was devoted to a caricature of Welk dancing with a little old lady, while another swooned in the background, and giant champagne bubbles floated from his baton. The caption read: "SIMPLE PLOWBOY is how bandleader Lawrence Welk describes himself. But he's far from the country bumpkin that his public image suggests. At 71, Welk, who brings his band to the CNE Grandstand this Monday, says he will earn $3 million this year, most of it from syndicated TV show, which is seen on 251 stations by 39 million." The article, written by Frank Rasky, went on to explain that Welk would collect approximately $76,000 for his one-night stand at the Canadian National Exhibition, and stated:

> Welk, long reputed to be the Cornball's Cornball, the Squeezbox Guy Lombardo, the hick accordionist who specializes in the squarest music this side of Euclid, has composed a solo piece that consists of groovy riffs of Dixieland jazz.
>
> "Yes, Dixieland jazz," said Welk in a phone interview this week from his Hollywood office on Wilshire Boulevard.
>
> "You may find this hard to believe," he said, speaking in his slightly Germanic-accented, high—pitched voice. "But Dixieland jazz was always my first secret love."

Although the writer went on to blast Welk in no uncertain terms about the "simple plowboy" image he keeps projecting, while raking in millions, it really disturbed me that the paper had given him so much space when he wasn't scheduled to appear for another two days, while Buddy was appearing that very night with his big band, plus the next afternoon and evening, giving free concerts in the Bandshell. I leafed through the section carefully, looking for an article about Buddy, but I couldn't find anything. Not even a mention. Not one line. I simply couldn't believe it, so I went through the entire section again. There was an article about coming attractions at the CNE Grandstand, starting August 19, giving more space to Welk, then including Evel Knievel (August 20), Liza Minnelli (August 21), Helen Reddy (August 22), and other entertainers, all the way through to the final day, September 1, when the "Chicago" rock group came in. But not one word about Buddy Rich. It was probably the editorial policy of the paper to run articles about featured performers several days in advance of their appearance, which was logical, but then, apparently, there was no follow-up at all. If I had been a tourist in town for the weekend, and had to rely on the newspaper for information on what was happening that day at the CNE, I wouldn't even have known that Buddy Rich was on the schedule.

Then it occurred to me that maybe Buddy *wasn't* playing that night. Maybe I'd somehow screwed up the dates. I threw the paper down, went inside, grabbed the telephone book, dialed the Canadian National Exhibition and asked when the Buddy Rich band was scheduled to play.

"Four o'clock this afternoon," the woman told me, "and nine o'clock this evening."

"*Four* o'clock?" I glanced at my watch.

"Yes, sir. In the Bandshell. Admission is free."

"Can you tell me what time it is now?"

"Yes, sir. I have—three fifty-four."

I knew it was at least a half-hour drive by taxi to the Exhibition grounds, and the traffic would be heavy, so I'd blown it. For some asinine reason, I'd gotten it into my head that Buddy was playing at nine only, then two shows on Sunday. So I'd taken the early afternoon flight, giving myself plenty of time for a leisurely trip. Buddy had taken an earlier flight and, as I learned later, he'd gone straight from the airport to the Exhibition.

Well, screw it, I thought. The sun was coming out at intervals and it was nice and warm, so I decided to go up to the rooftop pool for a swim. I changed into swim trunks and a T-shirt, and when I got up there, the pool was closed. Well, screw it, I thought. I took the elevator down to the lobby, crossed Lake Shore Boulevard, and went for a stroll in Marine Park.

It was really very pleasant. I remember the long, wide stretch of deep-green grass, and trees heavy with leaves fronting on the calm lake, and scattered picnic tables with families, and literally thousands of ducks wandering around, completely free. The sun broke through the clouds for an extended period then, and I walked about a mile or so, all the way up to the public beach, then sat on the grass near the water and had a cigarette. The lake smelled like ocean water, and looked like an ocean, to the horizon. To the east, the distant downtown skyline was still hazy, but I could see a huge blimp that seemed to be floating in a stationary position to the far right of the CN tower. I didn't know it then, but the blimp was anchored directly above the Exhibition grounds.

I returned to the hotel about 5:30 and called Stanley's room again. He and Sandi had just returned from the concert and were resting; he asked me to meet them in the lobby at 6:15. I changed and had a snack in the hamburger joint next to the hotel, because I knew we probably wouldn't have dinner until long after the show.

When I went to the lobby at 6:15, Sandi was sitting alone by a window near the front desk, reading a newspaper. She was about thirty-five, a Canadian, and a former actress and model, with dark brunette hair, dark skin, hazel eyes, and a dynamite figure. That evening she wore a tight-fitting blue blouse and faded, belled Levi's with copper studs around the pockets and down the outside seams. As usual, she had attractive silver jewelry (never gold), mostly rings and bracelets, not overdone, just enough. She was just beginning to get serious about photography that summer, and had a genuine talent for it, and her Nikon F was on the seat beside her.

I pulled up a chair nearby. "What's a nice kid like you doing with an expensive camera like that?"

She glanced up smiling, then did a double-take when she saw my new T-shirt. It was green, with a bright yellow caricature of the one and only "Tweety-Pie" canary, from the one and only "Felix the Cat" cartoons. Sandi laughed out loud, an almost luxurious laugh.

"Thought I'd dress in keeping with the gravity of the situation."

"I knew it'd happen," she said. "I knew that if you hung around Buddy Rich long enough—"

"I'd fly like a yellowbird."

"—you'd go over the edge, and it's finally happened. That's why you didn't come to the concert, right? You were ashamed to be seen in public."

"Just couldn't get up enough courage."

"Yeah, well, actually, you missed some pretty hairy happenings," she said softly, with just a trace of her Canadian accent, which returned at odd times. "You wouldn't believe what we had to go through to get him in here."

"Buddy?"

"Buddy and Cathy. We came in on the early morning flight with Cathy, Beverly, Michele and Debby—Debby Thompson, she's the fourth member of the group, you haven't met her yet, she's been out sick. Buddy and Leo took the Air Canada flight from Kennedy at one o'clock. Well, we'd booked a suite for Buddy and Cathy, beautiful place, booked it weeks in advance. We check in, we go up to see his suite, to get Cathy all settled, right? It's occupied. Clothes all over, closets full, looked like some family had been there for weeks. And no other suites available, of course, because of the Exhibition. Not even a *room*. Completely booked."

"Delightful."

"Right? So Stanley goes down to the office, tries to be diplomatic, and this is about one thirty, Buddy's due in another hour. And there's just no way. Absolutely no *way* they can get those people out of there in time. They'd been granted a late check-out so they could attend the Exhibition!"

I smiled. "Oh, well, Buddy would've understood *that*."

"Oh, of course."

"He would've just smiled sweetly and said, 'Well, that's life.'"

"Of course. Anyway, we had to play it by ear and wait for the people to return, so Stanley arranged for Buddy and Leo to go directly from the airport to the Bandshell. The excuse was that it'd be much more convenient that way. Buddy still doesn't know what happened."

"Would've been fun, huh?"

She looked at me cross-eyed.

"I can just see Buddy discussing the idea with the hotel manager."

"Over tea," she said.

"Sitting on his suitcases in the lobby."

About 6:45, Buddy finally came down with Leo, Stanley, and the girls, and when he saw my T-shirt and ragged old jeans, he went through a whole number—leaning against the front desk, pointing me out, laughing—but Cathy, Beverly, Michele, and Debby thought the shirt was cool as hell and wanted to know where I got it. I put on my dark sunglasses and smirked at Buddy.

"You'll *need* those shades, man," he told me.

One of the desk clerks, a young blonde girl, held out an autograph book to him. "Are you Buddy Rich?"

He became serious instantly. "No, I'm not."

"Oh, I'm—sorry."

"I'm his manager."

"Oh." She smiled, then glanced at Stanley, Leo, and me.

"That's him over there," Buddy said.

"Which one?"

He pointed to me. "The man with the sunglasses and the canary on his shirt. The one surrounded by all the girls."

She looked over at me uncertainly.

"He's got a new hairpiece," Buddy said. "Makes him look a lot younger, you know?"

"Oh, yes, now I recognize—"

"It's a new, young image," he said, still quite serious. "We worked a long time on it. What do you think?"

I was talking with Cathy and Michele, but I heard almost every word he said, and I knew Beverly and Debby heard him, because they broke into our conversation and started to call me Buddy, asking questions about the afternoon show. At that point, I knew I'd have to go along with it, but I seriously doubted that I could keep a straight face.

"Hey, *Buddy*," Buddy said loudly. "Come here a minute, I'd like you to meet somebody."

I managed to walk over nonchalantly, adjusting my sunglasses.

"Like you to meet—what's your name, honey?"

"Joan Sullivan."

"Hi, Joan, nice to see you," I said in my best, low, gravel-throated imitation. I shook hands with her. She looked scared as hell. That gave me the confidence I needed.

She handed me the autograph book and a pen, and when I saw that her hand was shaking I felt sorry for her but it was too late. By that time I was surrounded by the four girls, Stanley, Leo, Buddy, Sandi, and Gene Lew, the Canadian distributor for Groove Merchant Records, who had just arrived, and they were all clued-in and playing it to the hilt and digging it.

"Would you please inscribe it to me?" the girl asked softly. "To Joan Sullivan?"

"Be glad to." I scrawled something really dumb like, "To Joan Sullivan—With lots of love, Buddy Rich," in Buddy's bold handwriting.

"Thank you, Mr. Rich," she said.

"I think Joan deserves a kiss," Buddy told me.

Somehow, I knew, I just *knew* he'd do a number like that, and I felt a terrific urge to laugh. If I'd looked at Buddy's face then, even a fast glance, I wouldn't have been able to hold it in, so I leaned over the desk quickly and kissed the girl on the cheek. There were loud "Ohhhs" and "Ahhhs" from the group, and then Buddy escorted me to the door, followed by the others. At the door, two teenage girls were waiting with autograph books, holding them out to me. I'm sure they didn't know *who* the hell I was supposed to be, but they didn't want to miss a celebrity. I signed the books "Felix the Cat," and they seemed delighted, probably thinking I was a new American rock star. Buddy escorted me out into the warm evening, where two limousines were waiting at the curb.

"You *rat*," I said softly.

He burst out laughing, the way you heard him laugh only rarely, clapping his hands, stomping his foot on the pavement; as the others came through the door and heard him, they howled with laughter, and I joined them, letting it all out. Buddy was trying to say, "I think Joan deserves a kiss," but every time he tried, it broke him up.

Stanley and the girls and I piled into one of the limos—Stanley in front—and Buddy, Leo, Sandi, and Gene Lew went in the other. We drove east on Lake Shore Boulevard, with the sun throwing long shadows ahead (the threat of rain had vanished), and the lake sparkling to our right, dotted with sailboats, beyond the park. After a mile or so, we ran into very heavy traffic because of the many thousands of people heading for the Exhibition, and the going was relatively slow.

The girls rehearsed several of their numbers on the way, singing certain phrases over and over, trying to get the harmony just right. Although the group was originally formed as "Hendricks Getz Thompson Rich," it was the first time they had the whole act together, because Debby had injured her neck in an automobile accident just before they were to open at Buddy's Place in the spring. They were each twenty years old that year, attractive and talented, Michele and Debby black, Cathy and Beverly white, and it was fun to sit there and listen to them, to catch the vibrations. There was an excitement in their voices and eyes and gestures, and I remember thinking that the very idea of performing live with a big band before 10,000 people must be a real trip, no matter how old you are, no matter how much experience you have, no matter how much you've got to gain or lose.

As we neared the CNE grounds, the congestion was almost unbelievable, with masses of Canadian police lost in a sea of people, cars, and buses, a crowd of more than 200,000 that particular night, fanning out over 350 acres, including one and one-half miles of lakeshore. What had once been a French trading post, 1749-1759, under the sovereignty of Louis XV, and later the scene of heavy fighting in the War of 1812, was now the kaleido-scopic locale of the largest annual exhibition in the world, in its ninety-sixth year that summer, and destined to draw 3.5 million people in its twenty days of operation.

When we passed the intersection at British Columbia Road, we could see the Carlsberg Festival beyond the fence to our left, then the Spain Exhibit, the Scadding Cabin, and, beyond the Rose Garden, the back of the huge white Bandshell was clearly visible. Our driver turned left toward the Prince Edward Island Crescent, stopped at the gate to show the guard our pass, and we proceeded very slowly, bearing left on the crescent, through the large crowd surrounding the Better Living Center & World of Women. Cars weren't normally allowed inside the grounds, and our driver had to keep tapping his horn all the way. People turned, surprised, and peered inside our two limos, as if looking for royalty.

We reached the stage door of the Bandshell before eight o'clock, and about fifty or sixty people were waiting there, young and old, with autograph books and cameras. As soon as we stopped, both cars were surrounded, then there was a rush for Buddy's car as he stepped out. I couldn't even see him at first, and there was some yelling and pushing, with flashbulbs going off, but when people realized that he wasn't going to run for the door, the atmosphere was more relaxed. He signed autographs calmly, talking and joking, and posed for pictures with people. That lasted for around fifteen minutes, with Leo doing his subtle maneuvering of Buddy closer and closer to the stage door, and then some middle-aged woman blew the whole mood.

"Mr. Rich, were you at Gene Krupa's funeral?" she asked loudly.

I saw Buddy pause in the middle of an autograph, just a beat, as if he'd forgotten something; then he finished, handed the book back to a youngster and accepted another book.

"Would you sign it to Charley Bradley, please?"

"Sure thing."

"Excuse me, Mr. Rich," the woman said, even louder. "Were you at Gene Krupa's funeral?" She wore very dark, oversized sunglasses.

He didn't look up. "Yes, I was."

"When was that—last October?"

He nodded, handed the book back, took another.

"Will you inscribe it to Judy, please?"

"You bet."

"And that was in New York, right?" the woman continued.

I remember the way he glanced at her, sideways, as he was signing the book He returned it and was handed a program.

"To Cathy—with a C, please?"

"Cathy with a C, that's how my daughter spells her name."

"I know. Is she performing with the new group tonight?"

"I hope so. If we can ever get inside."

"Mr. Rich," the woman persisted. "Was it in New York, the funeral?" I could see Buddy's reflection in her dark sunglasses.

"That's right," he said, almost inaudibly.

"Well, I heard his body was moved to Chicago."

He returned the program, accepted a small scrapbook opened to a page with his picture. "Hey, that's very nice."

"Would you please make it to Barbara and Carol?"

"You got it."

"Why was Krupa's body moved to Chicago?" the woman asked.

Buddy finished signing the scrapbook, turned to the woman, took a deep breath, spoke quietly. "Do you realize you're talking about one of my best friends?"

"Certainly," she said, Buddy's image big in her glasses. "All I'm asking is why his body was moved to Chicago."

"Lady, I don't want to talk about it."

"Is that such a big deal, to ask a simple question?"

He looked at her, blinking, seeing his double reflection.

"Was that his hometown, Chicago?"

Somebody tried to hand him another autograph book, but he pushed it away gently and headed for the stairs to the stage door.

"Well, I'm sorry, I apologize," the woman called after him. "Don't you think you're making a big thing out of nothing?"

Buddy stopped with his hand on the railing, shoulders hunched, then turned quickly and started toward her.

Leo blocked his way, something I'd never seen him do before, saying, "Come on, B, forget it, cool it, she doesn't understand," and then Stanley appeared out of nowhere, blocking the way, shouting: "Get her out of here! Get that woman the hell out of here!"

The woman didn't budge. "What's the matter with him, anyway, is he sick or what?"

"Lady," Buddy said, his voice thick, "you're the one who's sick. You and everybody like you. You don't *care* about people. You don't *care* about the feelings of other people. You didn't care about Gene when he was *alive*, when he *needed* people to care, and you obviously don't care about *me*, about *my* feelings. Because you're oblivious to people. Sick? You're the one who's sick. And the saddest part is, you don't even know it."

7

SUNDAY MORNING WAS bright and warm, hardly a cloud in the sky, and from the rooftop pool you could see literally hundreds of sailboats on Lake Ontario, all the way east to the blimp hanging lazily over the Exhibition grounds. Directly below, the wide lanes of Lake Shore Boulevard sparkled with the colorful tops of toylike cars. By the time Stanley and Sandi joined me, about 10:30, three or four families had taken over the pool, all Canadians, and the children were having a hell of a good time. We sat on deck chairs in the corner and put on a lot of sun cream, because the sun was very strong. Sandi wore a bikini, and she sure had the figure for it, despite the twelve-course dinner we'd had the previous night, courtesy of Gene Lew. He'd taken our whole group to his favorite Chinese restaurant after the show, sat us at a long table, and really laid it on.

"How about that tea last night?" I asked Sandi.

"Best tea in Chinatown."

"What tea?" Stanley asked. "What're you guys talking about?"

Sandi and I exchanged glances, then laughed.

"Not booze," Stanley said, "I know that, 'cause they don't have a liquor license, Gene told me that."

"Remember that silver teapot?" I asked him.

"Yeah. What'd he—?"

"Remember how Sandi and I kept pouring that stuff out?"

"*That's* why you were laughing all night!"

"Yeah!"

"Hidin' it," he said. "*Sneakin'* it."

"That's when you really enjoy that stuff, Stanley."

"Yeah," Sandi said. "Sneakin' it. In a teacup."

Stanley shook his head. "No. No, I can't buy that, because you weren't drunk. See, I know when Sandi's had a couple of drinks, I can tell that, because she gets silly."

I looked at Sandi. "Can't put anything over on him, right?"

"No way. Like, he still doesn't believe I was born in a place called East Angus."

"East *Angus*?"

"Yeah."

"Oh, East Angus," I said seriously. "That's—actually, that's a famous city in Canada, Stanley, that's where all the famous Aberdeen Angus cattle come from. You know, the beautiful hornless cattle with the smooth black coats?"

He nodded. "I'll tell you something. Maybe I was born on East Houston Street, but even *I'm* not *that* dumb!"

Sandi and I laughed; it was his expression.

"Aberdeen Angus cattle," he said.

"Know why they're hornless?" Sandi asked him.

"Don't tell me, let me guess."

"They've got them on a special diet," she said.

"Yeah, huh?"

"Chinese-Canadian tea," she told him.

"Spiked with saltpeter," I added.

Stanley threw his towel down, ran to the pool and leaped over the edge, making his legs run faster in midair, yelling like a madman before he hit the water. Straight out of Laurel and Hardy. Sandi and I laughed hard, especially when we saw that he'd splashed the hell out of two middle-aged women sitting nearby. When he came up and saw the dirty looks, he swam underwater to the other end of the pool.

"East *Angus?*" I asked Sandi.

"It's a little lumber town in the eastern townships, in the province of Quebec, which is about—I'd say a hundred miles from Montreal. I went to a one-room schoolhouse and all. Then we went to Montreal, and my father pulled himself up on his own and became treasurer of International Paper. From a lumberjack to treasurer of International Paper. Then, in Montreal, I guess we lived there for a couple of years, until my parents bought a house in the suburbs. After that, well, I got married very young. Much too young."

"How old were you?"

"Eighteen."

"How long did it last?"

"About five years. I didn't even know I was being divorced until I got the final papers."

"How did a girl from East Angus meet a guy from East Houston Street?"

Sandi smiled, leaned back in the deck chair, sweating nicely in the sun, her eyes closed. "Three days after my visa was final. I got my visa to come to the States to work, and I was staying with a girlfriend of mine. She was going up to watch some friends of hers, guys, they were playing touch football in Central Park. And I was down in the dumps and she talked me into going along. And I hated football, I had no interest in going, but I went. And Stanley was one of the guys playing. I remember, I got there just after he fell and hit his head and blacked out for a few minutes. I keep accusing him, I keep saying, 'If you ever fall and hit your head again, and that same thing happens, you'll wake up and you won't remember any of this.'"

I laughed. "What a perfect out—'I hit my head, I didn't know what I was doing.'"

"Right. And we met—actually, it started out that—I don't know how interested he was, but I didn't really pay that much attention to him at first. Then he came over and sat down beside me and started talking, and I think we talked about the theater. And I had never been to the theater in my life, I had never done any of these things, and New York was like a real trip to me then. I kept walking around with my head up, looking at all the skyscrapers. He offered to take me to see all these various concerts, he was manager of 'Hines, Hines and Dad' then. He took me to a concert they were doing, and he was conducting the orchestra. And we went to plays and I really loved it. We started off just being really good friends, you know, and it just went from there. We went together for about two and a half years before we got married."

"Were you working then?"

"I was acting. I came to New York originally to do a television special. I'd been a model in Montreal for about five, six years. When I came to New York, it was to act in this television special. Then I got interested in film editing, and I started to work on the same film that I was acting in, and I learned a lot."

"What was it?"

"It was a thing called *Paradox*, and it never went on the air. They couldn't find a sponsor. Terrific ideas, but it never made it on the air. I still have the outtakes at home—in thirty-five millimeter."

"Thirty-five millimeter!"

"Yeah!" She laughed, opened her eyes.

"All you need now is a theater."

She shrugged, sat up, smiled. "They told me that I was finally learning to be a good editor when they found pieces of myself on the cutting-room floor."

Although I knew it would be a long day at the Exhibition, with Buddy giving an afternoon and evening concert, I could hardly wait to get out to the grounds. I wanted to see everything in daylight, go on some of the wild rides, buy some of the far-out T-shirts that were on sale all over the place, hang around the midway and watch all the people, and generally get the feel of the Exhibition. I knew Buddy, Leo, and the girls would sleep late, so I convinced Sandi and Stanley to go out with me in the early afternoon. We took a cab and arrived about 1:30 and there was already an enormous crowd.

When we went in through Princes' Gates, I bought a program and we looked up the scheduled events for that day. There were over thirty major ones, but from 1:30 to 4, when Buddy's concert started, we had our choice of the CNE Karate Championships, the Canadian Powerlifting Championships, the Band of the Carabinieri, the Hell Drivers, the Aquarama Water Show, and the Pony Society Futurity. They were spread out over miles, so we decided to just wander around for a while. We walked up Princes' Boulevard, with the Alpine Way cablecars overhead, past Kiddieland and the Bulova Tower, and when we reached the Mile-and-a-Half Midway, Sandi and I decided we absolutely had to get on some of the rides. At that point, Stanley remembered that he had some unfinished business to transact somewhere, anywhere, so we agreed to meet him at the Bandshell before Buddy's show.

I bought a couple of coupon books (you needed coupons for every ride), and as we were waiting in line for "The Munster," which was the most dangerous-looking ride we could find, I read the back of one of the coupons out loud to Sandi: "The management is not responsible for accidents, and, in accepting this coupon, the holder thereof agrees to participate at his or her own risk."

Sandi looked at me, then we both looked at the huge machine in action. It had about twelve octopus-like arms, each holding a number of little capsules of people, and the arms whirled in a circle while shooting up and down and in and out, all at gradually accelerating speeds, with the capsules themselves spinning independently, and timed to just miss one another every few seconds. All this to loud acid-rock music. As maximum speed was achieved, you could hardly hear the music over the blood-curdling screams.

"The, uh, the line's pretty *long*!" I shouted.

She nodded.

"We don't have too much *time*!"

She nodded.

"Oh, hell, let's look at the *T-shirts* first, then we can come *back*!"

Somehow, walking around in the warm sun after that, I felt strangely elated. Cowardly, but elated. T-shirts were really the rage at the Exhibition, young and old wore them, and there were booths all over devoted to them. You could have them custom-made in minutes, with virtually any combination of words and graphics pressed on by special decal machines. After looking for about half an hour, I found one ready-made that was perfect for Buddy. It had large letters arranged around a circular logo: MARIJUANA PICKERS LOCAL UNION NO. 13, with a big green marijuana leaf in the center. I thought it was so cool that I bought the same shirt in two sizes, medium and small, just to be sure. We selected several other T-shirts for ourselves, including one with a cartoon of "The Road Runner" for me, which I changed into on the spot. And we finally went on two relatively tame rides, in preparation for "The Munster," which we agreed to try after the concert.

By the time we passed behind the 20,000-seat Grandstand, where the Hell Drivers were performing before what sounded like a good crowd, it was about 3:45. We were reasonably close to the Bandshell then, but we stepped up our pace. Crossing the Prince Edward Island Crescent, we could see about a dozen members of Buddy's band already on stage, tuning up. As nearly as we could tell, all 10,000 wooden seats were occupied and the overflow crowd was beginning to fill the grassy areas around, with some young groups having picnics.

Backstage, Buddy's dressing room was empty, so we hurried to the stage-left wing. He was there with Leo and Stanley, but they weren't talking, and I picked up the vibrations of another one of Buddy's moods. He was leaning against the edge of the wing, looking out at the crowd. I remember feeling strangely moved, wondering how many thousands of times he had stood in the wings like that, over a career of more than fifty years, gazing out at audiences long before he had even reached the age of reason. I had read all of his scrapbooks by then, studied all of the actual newspaper reviews, dating back over fifty-six years, and knew it wasn't any press agent's hyperbole. In May, 1918, at the age of eighteen months, he played *Stars and Stripes Forever* before his first vaudeville audience; at three, he was a permanent part of his parents' act, "Wilson and Rich," essentially blackface comedy; at seven, he was a single, billed as "Traps" the Drum Wonder, dressed in a sailor suit and with long curly hair, working the circuits across the country and abroad, the second highest paid child star in the world, surpassed only by Jackie Coogan. Looking out at audiences: Because his grade school lessons were mailed to him every week—five lessons to a package—and returned to school authorities promptly, completed for the most part by his father and a tutor; for if Buddy failed, the act folded, and the money dried up. Looking out at audiences: Because his father knew the legal ropes, and they rarely stayed in one city long enough to be prosecuted under the various child labor laws.

Looking out at audiences: Until he "retired" from vaudeville at the age of fourteen, with virtually no formal education, and the permanent damage had been done.

Looking out at audiences: As he was doing now, sizing them up. studying their faces, maybe even envying them. And, with that inward gaze, wondering, maybe, how many years he could go on doing that.

I have a present for you," I told him.

He turned. "Yeah? Well, I hope so."

I whipped out the T-shirt and one quick glance made him smile. He compared both sizes, grabbed the medium, ran back to his dressing room. When he came back, he was laughing, the shirt looked fantastic, and the change in mood was complete.

Minutes later, he was announced, and walked out on stage, arms spread wide, showing the audience his shirt with exaggerated pride, strictly vaudeville, but hilarious, and the response was a tremendous roar of approval that began in the first ten or twenty rows and swept back in waves, as word spread to those who couldn't read the words, followed by loud and enthusiastic applause. He turned to the sixteen-member band, spread his arms, bowed very formally from the waist, and really broke the guys up. Photographers rushed to the edge of the stage and began shooting like crazy as he turned around again, this time bowing to the crowd. It was just one of those spontaneous moods that hit him from nowhere, turning on an entire concert, and I remember thinking that a sight-gag costing hundreds of dollars probably wouldn't have come close to getting that kind of reaction.

But I have to admit that it was bewildering to me, too, that the change of a T-shirt could trigger such a dramatic change in the man. The only frame of reference that came to mind was my observation of children who would be sulking or crying one minute, and then, given something novel to distract them, would smile or laugh the next. I sat cross-legged at the side of the stage and watched, as Buddy left the microphone, bounded up the steps to his drums, gave the downbeat, then threw back his head and laughed out loud as the music exploded around him. And, to be honest about it, I envied him that flexibility. Looking back, I suppose I was just beginning to realize something vital to an understanding of the man: That Buddy Rich, like many gifted people I've known, had somehow built up an immunity to the peculiarly human, extremely contagious, invariably progressive, and ultimately fatal disease of *sophistication*. At times, there was something distinctly "childlike" about him, and I mean that in the true sense of the term. He had somehow retained the ability to feel and act instinctively, as most children do before they're educated out of it; to follow his intuition and natural curiosity; and, most importantly, to use his imagination, which had translated itself into his work.

Why he retained these qualities, during a childhood spent almost exclusively with adults, is the question nobody seems capable of answering. Yet, one of the scrapbooks contains an early interview that gives at least some insight. It appeared in a New York newspaper (unidentified) in 1922, and the child's face in the photograph, looking out at me then from a distance of fifty-one years, could be the face of almost any five-year-old American boy—long, thick hair over his forehead and ears, a bright-looking kid with a pleasant expression, obviously posed but not pretentious, a face bearing absolutely no resemblance to the man I knew, not the slightest trace, not even in the eyes and mouth.

DRUM STAR AT
AGE OF FIVE

Traps Making a Hit
at Pantages; Is
Regular Boy

BY DAISY HENRY

A FOLLIES STAR at the age of 5. How would you like to be able to boast such a reputation? Pretty nice, we think.

At the Pantages this week, one of the brightest spots of the bill is the appearance of "Traps,"

a 5-year-old youngster, who plays the drums in a manner that would make many grownups of his profession green with envy.

"Traps'" real name is Bernard Rich. His mother and daddy have been in the theatrical business for 20 years. Just now, Mamma Rich is at home taking care of a new little brother, and daddy and Bernard, who are real pals, are traveling the Pantages circuit.

"Traps" chose his own profession when a mere baby. Rhythm ought to be his middle name, for at the tender age of one year and a half, this tot made his first appearance at the end of his parents' act. "Before 'Traps' ever went on stage, he used to stand in the wings at the theater and beat time while his mother was singing or dancing—in fact, his first pair of drumsticks was a baby knife and fork, with which he was wont to beat time on the dining table," his dad told me when I called backstage Wednesday afternoon.

Raymond Hitchcock borrowed "Traps" at the age of 3 for a specialty in his "Pin Wheel" show, and one year later he was incorporated into the Follies show. A $40,000 toy shop setting was built for the youngster in the Follies production and he made a tremendous hit.

"Traps" doesn't confine his talents to drum playing, either. His little monologue with his daddy reveals an acting ability, too.

When I first spied "Traps" backstage, his eyes were filled with tears, but he checked them back gallantly to run out and take several bows. The youngster had accidentally caught his tiny finger between the sticks and the drum while winding up Sousa's "Stars and Stripes."

"Do you like playing the drums, 'Traps'?" I asked him, while his daddy wiped away his tears.

Mr. Rich answered for "Traps," "You bet he does, better than anything else."

"'Cept cherries," piped up "Traps." It seems daddy had a bag of cherries in the dressing room.

As I left the backstage lobby and glanced into the youngster's dressing room, I spied a tiny golf bag, fully equipped with driver, brassie, midiron, mashie and putter. Also, baseball mitts and a tennis racquet, which furthers my opinion that the youngster and his daddy are great pals, and that "Traps'" ability to put such a display of feeling into Sousa's "Stars and Stripes" is because he is a real American boy.

Obviously, whatever Buddy was back then, he wasn't the real American boy that reporter Daisy Henry thought she observed in that brief backstage visit. But, for me, it was an intriguing glimpse into the unusual—and complicated—relationship between Buddy and his father, Bob, a glimpse that occurred infrequently in the scrapbooks. The relationship was to continue for an exceptional length of time, by most standards, for Bob Rich was still very much alive and alert that summer, at eighty-seven. I had met him at the club and I knew, almost from the beginning, that I could probably depend upon him to answer questions about Buddy that nobody else could possibly answer. He seemed to be able to rattle off names, dates, cities, theaters, and details about Buddy's career with considerable ease, particularly things that had happened forty or fifty years ago, although he was a little uncertain about events over the past ten or fifteen years. So I was looking forward to long talks with him, which we eventually had and enjoyed, for the most part. Yet, in retrospect, I'm certain that I had no conception of how vivid the memories would be for him, how deeply he felt about them, how he cherished them to the exclusion of almost everything else in his life, and how painful some of the recollections would actually be.

Those experiences would come only too soon, within the next few weeks. But that afternoon at the Exhibition, the fifty-six-year-old Buddy Rich was at the top of his form, in high spirits all the way, and the big band reflected his mood to a man, giving a superb, upbeat, inspired performance. The crowd loved "Hendricks Getz Thompson Rich," although they really didn't have their act together yet, and Buddy clowned around with them before and after their numbers, to the delight of the photographers. The concert built up to, and ended with, *West Side Story*, and Buddy's solo had to be one of the best I'd ever seen.

Afterward, the scene was totally bizarre, starting with the predictable standing ovation, which quickly spawned a running, shouting mob of young people—probably several hundred, although it seemed like a lot more at the time—headed toward the stage in the bright sun, and I remember jumping to my feet, not knowing quite what to expect. Within seconds, three uniformed policemen were out on stage, hurrying to the edge, along with the MC, and if they hadn't appeared, I'm sure that mob would've been all over the stage—and all over all of us. But the mob's momentum was stopped at the apron, where the first wave of them got shoved hard against the stage, and I remember the telescope effect as they swarmed together and the hundreds of young faces and the sea of hands reaching to touch Buddy's as he came forward. He started at the far end, bending, crouching, sometimes getting down on one knee, reaching to high-five the closest hands, straining to touch the others, laughing, moving as quickly as he could from one end of the stage to the other, while the shouting continued. When he finally got over to my end, one teenage boy held on to his hand and yelled something to him; whatever the kid said, Buddy seemed to dig it, and came off stage laughing.

Leo, Stanley, Sandi, and I followed him into the shade of the wings. He opened his right hand and showed us a joint of marijuana.

"How *about* these cats!" he said.

"What happened?" Sandi asked.

"Kid gave him a *joint*," Stanley said.

Buddy nodded quickly; his eyes had filled, as they often did when he was very happy. "Know what the kid said?" Says, 'You got a lot of friends here.'"

After showering and changing in the dressing room, Buddy taped an especially good interview with Lewis Markowitz of Radio York (York University), a young guy who really knew what jazz was all about, and I asked the sound technician, Bruce Wood, if I could have a copy of the tape. He agreed, took my name and address, but he wouldn't take any money for it.

Buddy was really turned-on that whole afternoon. After signing autographs outside the stage door, he piled our group into the two limos and we took off for Ontario Place, a tiny peninsula south of the Exhibition grounds, where he had reservations for two helicopter rides around the downtown area. Buddy, Cathy, Leo, and

Beverly went up first (Cathy and Beverly had never been on a helicopter and were very nervous), then Stanley, Sandi, me, and a man we didn't know. The pilot was a woman and it was a pleasant fifteen-minute flight around the tall CN Tower, with a great view of the city and, on the way back, the entire Exhibition grounds, which seemed to stretch on forever. Looking down at a moving crowd of more than 200,000 people, from a relatively low altitude, is a trip you don't forget in a hurry.

When we got back to the Bandshell and went off in a group to check out the sights, I remember how excited Cathy was, leading us down the midway in the sun, dancing, singing, snapping her fingers, and her enthusiasm was really contagious. As usual, I found it difficult to take my eyes off her, and I admit that without any kind of qualification. It was just the plain, simple truth. That summer, at twenty, Cathy was so attractive that you found yourself staring at her. Which was not so unusual, really, but if you knew her, you understood that it was much more than a physical attraction; it was something you sensed, something about her personality, something you couldn't quite define. Relatively tall, a bit awkward then, with her dark hair worn fairly long, and with very little makeup, she was inclined to underplay the "feminine" aspect, like most girls her age, and to wear the "neuter" clothes so popular that year. But no amount of camouflage could hide the vivaciousness that was so much a part of her, the happy feeling she generated, the spontaneous sense of humor. You had the unmistakable impression that she was in love with the possibilities of life, and intended to get a big chunk of it, despite the odds. How do you teach that attitude? Where does it come from? Did Buddy have it at that age? Did Marie? And how long does it last?

We stopped at a T-shirt stand. Cathy looked them all over carefully, finally selected one with a Canadian flag on top, then asked the man to press on the word "Cookies" below the flag.

"*Cookies?*" I asked.

"Yeah. It's—sort of a private joke."

"I can keep a secret."

Her dark eyes glanced sideways to see if Buddy was listening. "The thing is, Jimmy's dog just—that's the guy I'm going with, Jimmy Mauelen, you know him, he used to play conga in the band? Jimmy's dog just goes absolutely bananas when you say 'cookies.' It means *food*, you know? We say it just before we feed him—'*Cookies, cookies!*'—and he jumps up and down and barks and goes crazy."

"Who, Jimmy?"

She burst out laughing, an all out laugh, and pushed me away.

"He must look ridiculous," I said. "Jumping up and down and barking."

The man behind the counter gave her the finished T-shirt. She showed it to Beverly and me, smiled, put it in the bag quickly, and paid the guy.

"Why the secrecy?" I asked.

Beverly answered for her: "Like, Buddy doesn't exactly see eye-to-eye with Jimmy. At least, not yet. Know what I mean?"

"Ahhhh," I said.

"*Ahhhhhh*," they harmonized.

There was a long line waiting for the roller-coaster (not "The Munster," thank God), but Stanley used a little influence and arranged for Buddy to go on immediately, with three others. Buddy and Cathy sat in the last car, and Beverly and I took the car directly in front of them. It was a wild ride, with sharp turns, steep inclines, and sudden plunges, and I remember Cathy and Beverly screaming, particularly Cathy. When we finally returned to the starting position, the girls and I got out in a hurry, dizzy and moaning, but Buddy walked calmly up the attendant and asked: "Hey, man, when does your ride start?"

It went like that and we all had a ball. Buddy called it quits about eight o'clock and walked back to the Bandshell with Stanley; Leo had somehow gotten lost in the crowd, which was very easy to do. Cathy, Beverly, Sandi, and I went on some more rides, including "The Munster," which was just as terrifying as it looked, and after that we decided to cool the rides, because Cathy and Beverly had to sing that night and they were already starting to lose their voices.

We wandered around in the warm August twilight, enjoying the whole thing, almost mesmerized by the steady stream of people, voices, sights, colors, and music, finally heading in the general direction of the Bandshell, but somehow oblivious to time. We were crossing the Crescent when we heard the band blast into its first number. Cathy shouted, "*Shit!*" to no one in particular; Beverly yelled, "*Oh, shit!*" They yanked off their shoes and sprinted toward the lighted Bandshell in the distance as the crowd roared its approval of the first few bars of *Chameleon.*

That night the band played to another SRO audience and, after *West Side Story*, there was another standing ovation and another large group of youngsters rushed in waves to the stage, where they were met at the edge by five police officers this time. I will never forget the loud, determined, rhythmic chant from the crowd, 10,000 voices shouting in unison from the warm darkness: "*More!—More!—More!*" And the sea of young faces and hands— red and yellow and blue in the spill of the footlights—and the staccato flashes of cameras, and Buddy, soaked with sweat, face dripping, bending, straining, kneeling, throwing high-fives with both hands, working his way from one side of the stage to the other again. As the chant continued, he took the microphone and tried to explain that he had to catch an eleven o'clock plane to New York, which was true, but when he walked offstage, waving, saluting, the chant continued from the darkness, even louder, more persistent by far, as if convinced by experience that they could persuade him by sheer tenacious repetition.

Buddy followed Leo backstage, changing his shirt on the run, wiping his face with a towel, ready for his fast shower. At the little-used stage entrance that was actually a loading platform, a single limo was waiting, motor running, headlights on full, back doors opened, Cathy and Beverly inside. Buddy and Leo ran down the steps, jumped in, doors slammed, the limo took off, tires squealing.

Stanley had to go to the bank in the International Building to collect the second half of the weekend's payment for the sixteen band members, and Sandi and I went with him. It was a relatively large amount of money and he took it in cash, U.S. currency, in order to pay the musicians before they left in the morning. I remember he carried the money in a big leather purse with a shoulder strap and, as we walked back to the Bandshell, his left hand gripped the purse at his side so tightly that his knuckles showed white.

I walked close to him, on the money side. "You're not, uh, you're not *afraid* of anything, are you, Stanley?"

"Me? No." He said it fast, like a reflex."

"Didn't think so. You're so—relaxed."

He smiled. "Get off my back, huh?"

"No sweat," I said. "I'm a karate expert."

"That's too bad. I was counting on you to fight."

The second limo was gone and the bus had taken the band back to their hotel. Enormous crowds were moving slowly toward the exits and we knew it would be impossible to get a cab. We decided to wait for the band bus to return for the instruments, which were being packed backstage, and ask the driver to drop us off.

It was a lovely evening, with the breeze starting to come in from the lake, and the stars were out and seemed very bright and close.

We sat on a park bench on the lawn to the left of the still-lighted Bandshell, and talked about the weekend. Couples and families strolled past, looking tired but happy, carrying shopping bags and packages, heading for the gates. The breeze from the lake was cool and smelled pleasant. At 11:20 (I checked my watch), we heard, and then saw, a jet streaking overhead, its slow-flashing colored lights moving among the stars.

"Look, there's Buddy!" Sandi said.

We were all so tired and slaphappy that we stood up, waved, and shouted, "Good night, Buddy! Good night, Leo! Good night, Cathy! Good night, Beverly!" Two young couples walking past stopped, looked up, looked at us, looked up again, then back at us. Before moving on, they exchanged weird glances, which classified us as juiced, stoned, or nuts. We sat back and laughed, then waved good night to them, too.

Every evening at 11:30 sharp, there was a fireworks display, originating from Ontario Place, which signaled the official end of each Exhibition day, and that night it was genuinely beautiful. We stood up and watched colored rockets and flares of every size and description shooting up and blasting, and Roman candles exploding with sudden, tremendous force, spraying out showers of sparks and fireballs that detonated in rapid succession, lighting the sky in brilliant colors, then fading. All around us, the crowds stopped moving and talking. The display started slowly, then built gradually over a period of at least fifteen minutes. As the most spectacular events occurred, we could hear "Ohhhs" and "Ahhhs" in the distance.

It seems almost uncanny to me now, but as we waited there in the cool dark, seeing the bursts of color, hearing the delayed blasts, watching the long, dying streamers, my mind returned to my childhood, and to my father, who used to take my two sisters and me out to watch far less flamboyant fireworks displays in the fields of my hometown, Albany, New York, usually on the night of the Fourth of July. And I remember the anticipation, and the excitement, and then the inevitable feeling of sharp disappointment when it was over, for nothing could possibly have lived up to my fantastic imaginings. As a child, I always expected too much of people. I think my father knew that and understood, although we never talked about the stuff of our dreams. We never talked about the invisible things, the questions without any answers, the doubts that made us bleed. In the deepest part of him, my father believed he was a failure, because he didn't make a lot of money, and I didn't know how to tell him that he was a success. I didn't know how to tell him that I loved him, and I've regretted it, terribly, all my life.

And then I was thinking about Buddy, and wondering if he felt the same way about his father, when Stanley turned to me, still looking up, his face reflecting the changing colors.

"I was thinking," he said. "This next week, you should try to talk with Buddy's father. Could be interesting, you know?"

I just looked at him.

"His father has a lot of the answers," he said softly. "But I'm afraid some of them aren't too pretty."

8

GETTING TO BRIGHTON Beach, Brooklyn, from midtown
Manhattan that summer, you took the IRT Lexington Avenue
express subway downtown from Grand Central to Fourteenth
Street, changed to the BMT line, and took the QJ train all the way
out. About forty-five minutes later, you rattled and swayed from
underground heat and darkness into hot, bright sunlight in south
Brooklyn and soon the tracks were elevated high over the little
communities that made up part of the "real" New York, a
completely different world from Manhattan. Brighton Beach was
the station just before Coney Island and the elevated tracks
extended directly over the main drag, Brighton Beach Avenue,
which was lined with hundreds of small stores—delicatessens,
groceries, poultry markets, pizza parlors, candy stores, laundries,
fruit stands, clothing stores, fish markets, Chinese restaurants,
bakeries, fast-food joints, bars, meat markets, and record stores
blaring rock. The sidewalks were crowded and there were a lot of
kids around that afternoon, many in swimsuits. Looking south,
down the narrow, shady, apartment-lined streets, you could see
the ocean. I knew the area well, because my aunt had been
confined to a nursing home nearby, and I visited her every week
during the summer of 1971, before she died.

Down in the hot street, I was again aware of the strong combination of smells and noise and music, which brought back
memories, but when the traffic light changed and I crossed the

street under the elevated tracks, it was shady and a little cooler. A subway train roared overhead, an express that didn't stop, and I remember the noise drowning out the music, and the patterns of sunlight flickering on the asphalt, and the vibrations.

Buddy's father lived just south of the elevated, on one of the streets leading to the sea, lined with attractive old apartment houses. The building, 3109 Brighton Seventh Street, was six stories of gray-brown brick, with a latticework of brown fire escapes down the front; I noticed how clean all the windows were in the clean brown frames, as if the residents took special pride in their building, and the white and gray stone arched entrance had tall double doors with glass so clean that it reflected my image like a mirror.

I took the elevator up, rang the bell, and heard footsteps approaching along a hallway. Bob Rich swung open the door, a relatively short man, completely bald, wearing black horn-rimmed glasses with lenses just thick enough to distort his dark eyes. He was smiling broadly, the kind of genuinely happy smile that could dominate his entire face, and often did, making his eyes squint and deepening the lines on his cheeks. But, unlike Buddy, he didn't show his teeth when he smiled. I could never decide if it was a conscious hiding of his teeth, or just the natural way he smiled, but it didn't make any difference. The smile alone made me feel instantly welcome before he said a word; he was obviously delighted to see me, although we hardly knew each other.

"John!" he said. "Come in, come in, what the hell took you so long?"

I shook his hand, then glanced at my watch. "I'm early!"

"Well, that's no excuse!" He laughed then, a quick, spontaneous outburst, still holding my hand tightly, looking up at me, his glasses catching the light, and I found myself laughing and looking forward to more of the same.

Louise, his second wife, walked down the hall toward us, an attractive, white-haired, gentle-looking woman. Her glasses had three-quarter frames and she was immaculately dressed in a white blouse and finely checked Chanel-type suit. Born in Paris, she had come to this country when she was seventeen, and still had traces of a French accent. At sixty-seven, she was twenty years younger than Bob. They had been married twenty-five years that month.

"You know Louise," he said. "The French bombshell."

She shook my hand and smiled. "We met at the club, yes. Don't pay any attention to him. He's gone crazy in his old age. Regression to adolescence, I think you call it."

The walls of the long hallway leading to the living room were completely covered with framed photographs and memorabilia, and Bob showed each of them to me before we went inside. Some were very old photos from his own vaudeville career, but the overwhelming majority covered Buddy's career, from the age of eighteen months to the present, like a one-man show at a gallery, photographs from all over the world, many of which I had never seen, and he identified virtually every person, the cities, countries, theaters, and approximate dates. I suppose he had recited the same information to so many people over the years that it wasn't really the astonishing feat of memory it seemed, but it was the way he did it that finally moved me, the gravel in his voice, the way he touched the glass of the frames ever so gently, the way he paused and looked up at me for my reaction, before moving on to the next picture. To the best of my knowledge, no one in my family had ever lived to be eighty-seven, and I don't think I had ever observed anyone of that age looking at a record of his life in frozen time, which is what photographs essentially are. Without them, how much would the mind actually recall in such vivid detail? How much would be lost? How much of time past would be rationalized? The written word can sometimes capture the ostensible quality of our lives, and even add a reflective dimension, which photographs cannot do, but how many of us have kept a written record? How many of us will be able to remember clearly what it was like to be young, and what we did, and who our friends were, and how we really looked, and how our children looked and changed over the years—without the aid of photographs, however posed, however amateur? I had always been attracted to photography for its singular capability to freeze time, but I left that hallway with a new optimism, after seeing the range of emotions it could actually recall in a person of that age, and especially the happiness.

The living room was small and comfortable, overlooking the street, and there were more photographs, of course. Louise served coffee and we talked easily and Bob wanted to know all about the concerts in Toronto and particularly about the documentary film that NBC News was going to shoot about Buddy that week, at the club and at a recording studio where he was cutting his new album. He was going to attend, he said, he wouldn't miss that for anything.

Later, he took me along on his daily constitutional stroll on the boardwalk. We walked south to Brighton Court where the swimming pool of the YM-YWHA was swarming with kids in the afternoon sun, crossed the street and turned left, past the clean, tan, three-story YM-YWHA building, then right on Coney Island Avenue and onto the enormous boardwalk, which extended for many miles, all the way to the amusement park at Coney Island, which we could see in the distance. To our left, the beach was really jammed, literally thousands of people, as far as you could see, and the glare of the ocean was very strong. The boardwalk, too, was crowded with people walking to and from the dozens of honky-tonk food and drink stands to our right. Bob used a cane, but said he only needed it to beat away the girls and autograph hounds. He wore a snappy red sport shirt and gray trousers, walked at a good clip, and seemed to enjoy the whole atmosphere.

"Buddy tells me your hometown is Albany," he said.

"That's right."

"That's *my* hometown!"

"Really? Albany, New York?"

"Yeah, I was *born* in Albany, grew *up* there. All my people're there, what's left of them. Ever hear of the Wanderers?"

"No."

"Did you know the Mendelsons?"

"Yes, I knew a family, the Mendelsons. Might not have been the same one. You remember the street you lived on?"

He looked at me as if I was crazy. "Certainly, *Broad* Street."

"Broad Street, of course, that's downtown."

"Broad Street, Clinton Street, Pearl Street, you name it. We had a store on Pearl. I was born in Albany, yeah, December second, eighteen hundred and eighty-six. Three months more, if I make it, eighty-eight years old I'll be. Eighty-eight years old."

"Eighty-eight. God."

He nodded, smiled the big smile.

"Where did you get into show business? In Albany?"

"I worked with a fella by the name of Reilly in Albany. We're playing—you know, clubs, little things, around. Five dollars a night apiece, things like that. And then, it was 'Rich and Reilly,' then."

"How old were you then?"

"I was about—I was a hoofer, strict dancing act, you know? I was about sixteen. And we went on there for a couple of years."

"Tell me about your father."

"My father? I couldn't."

"What do you remember about him?"

"Nothing."

"Was he born in this country?"

"I think he was born in Russia. My mother was born in— Austria."

"Did you go to school in Albany?"

"Yeah, went to Albany Business College, ABC."

"Oh, yes, ABC, I know ABC."

"Yeah, on the corner of North Pearl and—" He looked up, tried to remember the street, couldn't. "I graduated there."

"In those days, you could enter business college at a very early age, I know that."

"I graduated when I was about sixteen, somewhere in there. About the time I was eighteen, I came down to New York, myself, and I got a job as a bookkeeper for a paper-box firm. And the firm, they had a—you know, bookkeeper, stenographer, those days, were men. No women. And then I did a single for a very short time, as a hoofer. And then I met a fella by the name of Wilson, and it was 'Wilson and Rich' for about fourteen years."

'You started with Wilson when you were about nineteen?"

"Yeah, about eighteen, nineteen, somewhere in there. I got married, I wasn't quite twenty-one. I was married in August, nineteen hundred and six." He stopped, glanced up the beach toward the tall steel structure of the Coney Island parachute jump, closed down years ago because it was too dangerous, but never torn down. "And I was married forty-one years," he said very softly. "To Buddy's mother."

His voice had broken and I remember him standing there in the bright sun, adjusting his thick glasses, looking straight up the beach. It was the first time I had seen him like that and I didn't know how to help him. He looked small and alone.

"Would you like to sit down on a bench?" I asked softly.

He shook his head, didn't look at me.

"That sun is pretty strong, Bob."

He shook his head.

"Maybe we should sit down for a little while."

He started walking again, staring straight ahead. "Started with Wilson when I was about nineteen, yeah. We went with a burlesque show."

We walked in silence for a while.

"What did the act start out as?"

"Blackface comedy. Comedy, singing—those years, you had to do everything." He seemed to brighten at that memory, turned to me, smiled, and began gesturing with his hands. "If you got a job in a show and they wanted you to do a part, if they needed a Mick, well, they said, 'Can you do Irish?'" He broke into an excellent imitation of an Irish brogue: "And you'd say, 'Well, I can try it now, I'll tell ya that now, me lad, I'll be there if ya need me.'"

We both laughed. It was really good.

"You know, you had to do everything," he said. "If they wanted a Dutch act, you could do it. Whatever they wanted, you had to do. But the act was a blackface comedy act." He was silent again, looking down at his cane as he walked. "I was a funny man. Used to get a lot of laughs, too." He nudged me with his elbow and laughed at himself, and it got me laughing, too.

"When did you start traveling the circuits?"

"We went over the Sullivan-Considine circuit when I was, uh, let's see. About nineteen, I think. Along with Al Jolson, Jimmy Wall, Arthur Rigby—we were all blackface comedians. Wilson and I got—a hundred and a quarter for the team. Al Jolson got sixty dollars, single. We were getting more money each than Jolson. And we were all friends. Jimmy Wall—all minstrel men. I had a minstrel group. And we got along."

"How did the act change as you went along, as the years went by?"

"Listen, you didn't change. For years. The Keith office had three hundred and seventy theaters. Booking, they were all-week-stands. The Loews circuit, they started that split-week business. Three and four shows a day. Before that, you did two shows a day and that was it. You had a matinee performance and a night performance."

"Six days a week?"

"Seven days, six days. If the theater was open seven days, you worked seven days a week." He slowed his pace then, cleared his throat, stared ahead. "We were there the year of the earthquake, just about when it was over. We worked in tents."

"In San Francisco?"

"San Francisco. That was in nineteen—? I think it was nineteen hundred and six. I'm not sure now, it was somewhere in there. I miss dates and names sometimes, you know?"

"It's a long *time*," I said, laughing. "Sixty-eight *years* ago!"

He nodded, smiled. "Quite a while."

"Where, actually, was Buddy born."

"Buddy was born right here in Brooklyn. September thirtieth, nineteen seventeen. I was thirty-one when he was born. All my kids were born in Brooklyn—Margie, Jo, Buddy, and then Mickey."

"How did he get started on drums—I mean, why was it drums?"

"I don't know. It's a mystery. My wife and I, we were playing a date, I think it was somewhere in—Connecticut. And we had an Italian act. Two boys did it with us, a team, you know, doing a comedy act. And, you know, we were like a family. All shows were like a family then. And we were walking along, between two shows, and we passed a music store. And Buddy stopped." He stopped walking, pointed straight ahead. "And he looked into the window. And he said: 'Me *dum*! Me *dum*! Me *dum*!' I didn't know what the hell he was talking about, 'Me dum,' and he's pointing to the window."

"What age?"

"Oh, he wasn't—he was less than eighteen months, I know that. Couldn't speak clearly. And the boys were with us, you know, the two boys in the act. And one of them says, 'He wants a *drum*.' I said, 'Nah.' Then it occurred to me, we couldn't go to a restaurant with him unless they had music. Between shows, you'd go out and eat, and we had to go to a place that had music in it. And he'd take a knife and a fork and fool around with them—that's what we thought, that it was just fooling. And, first thing you know, the guys bought him a little toy drum. And he was in heaven."

He smiled all-out, remembering, and we started walking again.

"Who bought it for him?"

"This team, the boys that worked on the show with us. The way we used to do it on the road, he had no child life at all. Worked since he's—well, less than two years old. So I used to carry baseball gloves and all, and go out and pick up kids in each town, and we'd play in an alley or someplace, so he could play with kids. And he didn't go to any public school or anything, he went to a professional children's school, and he never attended that—maybe a few times—because we were on the road all the time. So they'd mail us the lessons and we'd do them. I'd teach it to him, and then have to send them in each week, and that had to be approved by the Board of Education. And they'd send report cards and the other lessons every week, and we'd have to do them. And when we were around here, I'd have a teacher come."

"A tutor?"

He laughed. "Oh, boy, you know, he would *fight* them, he didn't want to study. But we used to put great big cards along the walls, and he became attracted to those, and he learned to spell and everything. And his *teacher*!" He whistled. "It'd break her heart, every time she'd come to teach him, he'd fight her. And she'd come out, sometimes, crying that he wouldn't listen. But he—he got along okay." He looked up at me, raised his eyebrows. "He can spell his name now." Again, he burst out laughing, enjoying it.

"Going back to the time when he was given a toy drum," I said. "What happened after that?"

"We went—the American Music Hall, on Eighth Avenue and Forty-second Street—I guess that's before your time, isn't it?"

"I think so."

"That's torn down or something? I think there's a big bank building there now, Eighth Avenue and Forty-second Street. That was the American Music Hall, that was *the* pride of the Loews circuit, *the* house. We went to see a show, there was a band on there one time. And he was—oh, about fifteen, sixteen months old. And we went in to hear the band. We had two seats and he'd sit up on the arm of one seat and listen. And we're sitting there and watching the show, and the guy hits a blue note. Now, mind you, he's fifteen months old, no exaggeration—he jumps out of that seat and he says: 'Oh, bad *moogage*! Bad *moogage*!' I could—I could hardly believe it."

"When he played in front of his first audience, where were you, what city?"

"We were playing a house in Buffalo, the Lafayette in Buffalo. And his mother and I were doing an act together then. And he had a pair of sticks. While we were rehearsing, he sat on the floor, playing on the floor with the sticks. He was wearing rompers then, and he was really playing, following the music that we were rehearsing. Well, the manager was there and he says, 'Does he work in your act?' I says, 'No.' He says, 'Let him go on and do that with you this afternoon.' He says, 'The owner will be tickled to death, he loves kids.' So, what can I lose? I let him go on. We got a chair out on stage, and I brought him on, I walked on with him. I mean, he could barely walk, he was only eighteen months old, he wasn't firm yet. Walked him up to the chair and he got a footing and started to play *Stars and Stripes Forever*."

"On a regular drum?"

"On the *chair*! You know, with a wooden seat. And it was perfect, but he didn't know when to stop, so we fixed it up, so he knew that 'Bum da-da dum-bum—*bum-bum!*' was the end. So we put a tag—you call it a tag—after the number is over, and he recognized it, and played 'Bum da-da dum-bum—*bum-bum!* on the chair. The guy went crazy. Came back that night, he says, 'The owner went wild this afternoon. Wants you to try and get him to go on every show.' So I says, 'Well...' He says, 'I'll take care of you, don't worry.'" He turned, raised one eyebrow at me, laughed softly. "So we let him go on every show for the rest of the week, and at the end of the week, he gave me twenty-five dollars extra, for the kid."

"Was it still with the chair?"

"The chair, sure, we didn't have a regular drum. Not for quite a while after. So the following week we went to Niagara Falls, the same booking, you know? So we got in there and started to rehearse and the manager came backstage and he says, 'Kid working with you?' I says, 'No.' I says, 'What do you know about—?' He says, 'The guy from Buffalo called me up.' He says, 'Like to have the kid.' I says, 'No, my contract don't call for the kid in the act.' He says, 'I'll take care of him.' I says, 'Oh, that's different.'" He laughed, looked at me, touched my arm. "So, I mean, we never had to pay transportation for him, we never had to pay meals for him—because we'd order meals for us and he'd eat out of our plate, you know, or get an extra plate, that's all. So, everything was *found*. So we played about—oh, about six weeks that way, I think it was, and finally we got a letter from the office for the *big* route, you know?"

"You mean your booking agent?"

"Yeah, the booking agent. I wired back, I says, 'No. *Money*! If you want the kid as part of the act—*money*!' I asked for a hundred. They offered twenty-five. I settled for fifty. So we played the route and I figured—well, now we'll build him up, cut down on what we're doing, there's the money. So that's the way it went. We come in, I bought a tuxedo, and we're going to be high class, we're going to do just maybe five, six minutes, let him do the rest, you know? And I'll do a couple of gags with him."

"By this time he had a set of drums?"

He nodded. "By this time, we'd played a little town in upstate New York, I can't think of the name, and I knew the manager, and he had a little guy, a drummer. And he gave Buddy a little drum. We put this drum on a chair and he played it on a chair."

"This is still at about two years old?"

"He was getting up to three years then. And we played various places and then his first set of drums were given to him by the Ludwig company in Chicago, in exchange for using their name on a line of their drums. They called it the Ludwig 'My Buddy' drum outfit. It was strictly for kids and I think it sold for thirty-one dollars. But the drum set they gave *him* was a real good one, of course, and on the bass drum, which was almost taller than him, they had a big sign: 'Traps, the Drum Wonder,' and then, under that, 'Using Ludwig Drums.' I never had to buy drums for him. Never in his whole life. They were begging us to use their drums, all the big manufacturers."

"But Ludwig was actually his first set."

"Yeah, Ludwig was his first set. And, incidentally, when he was seven—and he was still with Ludwig—we went to Australia. We were playing some house in New Jersey and we heard that the booker from Australia was in town, and I wanted Australia. More for a buildup than anything else. We were with the Morris office then, so I went to the Morris office and I got ahold of Abe

Lastfogel, who was top man then; he's still chairman of the board now, I guess. The old man, William Morris, passed away long before that. And I saw Lastfogel, and they had just opened a new office, and I says, 'I want you to bring the Australian booker to the show tonight.' I says, 'I'll buy your dinner, I'll pay the taxi fare, I want him to cover the show tonight.' This was in Jersey. So he says, 'All right, I'll bring him over.' Brought him over, they saw the show; the next morning, called me up, 'Come over to the office.' Couple of days, I had a contract for Australia. Buddy was seven years old, Mickey was a babe in arms, his mother and I, they got transportation for all of us to Australia and back. And the highest paid single that ever was over there."

"That was nineteen twenty-four, so you had to go by ship."

"Oh, yeah, that was long before airline service."

"How long did it take to get there?"

"It took us twenty-one days from San Francisco to Sydney." He smiled at the memory. "Twenty-one days. That was the Spreckles Line, the sugar man, and the only other line was from Canada, a bigger ship, took nineteen days. We went over there, we had a contract for ten weeks out of twelve. We played *eighteen.* Six weeks in a house. Six weeks in Sydney, six weeks in Melbourne, then back to Sydney for another six weeks; that was eighteen, then we had two weeks in Brisbane. On the way back, we stopped off in Honolulu. We had six hours there, on the stopover, and we took a walk over to the theater and I saw the manager and he says, 'Yeah, I heard all about the kid from Australia.' I says, 'Can you use him?' He says, 'He can go to work tomorrow.' So we made a deal, I went over to the ship, had them get his drums and everything out of the hold, moved them over to the theater, and we stayed there—I think it was four weeks, I'm not sure."

We walked for a while without talking. I remember three girls in very brief bikinis passed in front of us, licking ice-cream cones.

Bob's head turned as we walked, following them to the other side of the boardwalk. He glanced at me, adjusted his glasses, and we both laughed softly.

"Something, huh?" he asked.

"Now I know why you take walks every day."

"Things like that keep up my *interest*."

I laughed, looked at his eyes, laughed again.

"And that's not *all*," he said, timing it just right.

"Eighty-seven years old…"

"Listen, don't let the numbers fool you." He broke into his fine Irish brogue: "It's all according to how ya feel, y'know. Sure, if the good Lord wanted us Albany lads to keep it down at eighty-seven years of age—why, he'd a splashed some water on the fire, now, wouldn't ya think? Ah, but the good Lord takes care of his own, don't he? Them with the map of Ireland all over their puss, I mean, we got it made in the shade, so to speak. Let's sit down and cool it a bit, what d'ya say to that?'"

We crossed to the ocean side of the boardwalk, glancing at each other, laughing softly, and then we had to walk about a hundred yards more before we could find an empty bench. The metal railing overlooking the beach was on a section of the boardwalk that had been repaired, a new section with new tan-colored boards. The next section, to our right, had the old blackened boards, followed by another new section, then an old one, the widest of all, in front of the food and drink stands. When you looked down between the slats, you could see kids on the sand below, sitting in the shade.

We finally found an empty bench and sat down. The wood was hot. I took out a pack of cigarettes, offered him one; he declined with a wave of his hand. We had a good view of the crowded beach through the railing.

"When did the name 'Traps' actually start?" I asked.

"The name started as soon as he went to work with us. On the chair."

"Who thought of it?"

"The name? I think I did. It was—you know, it was easy to remember. You had to have something—" he snapped his fingers—"quick, those days. Today, they got big, long, foreign names. Those days, they had to be short names—" he snapped his fingers several times—"everybody would know it, you know. Well, we made it 'Traps.' And he wore long hair, you know, Buster Brown, until he was about—eight years old, I guess. And, it's funny, we were walking along the boardwalk in Atlantic City. This is after Australia, about nineteen twenty-five, and we were playing the Keith Theater, Keith's Atlantic City. And we're walking along the boardwalk and a couple of kids—I can see it clearly—a couple of kids were coming toward us with their parents and they said, 'Oh, look at that *sissy* there!' And he heard it. And I looked at his face. And it was ashes. He was *hurt*. And I took him right off the boardwalk and went to a barbershop and trimmed his hair. And he was a *boy* then, you know? It broke his heart to hear them call him that."

"I've read that a lot of people thought he was a midget—they simply couldn't believe that a child could play that well."

"Oh, sure. When he was in the Follies, the owner of the French Line, the steamship company, just couldn't believe it. When Buddy opened, opening night at the Shubert Theater on Forty-fourth Street, the man had to come backstage to see for himself. The manager took him backstage after the show and he just stared at the kid and tried to talk with him. And Buddy would never talk to anybody, you know. He was *afraid*. He was afraid of people. And *women*—" he whistled—"women wanted to go over and grab him and hug him, and he got so scared of women that he was a big boy before he began to realize that he liked girls."

"He made up for lost time."

"Sure did," he agreed, laughing. "Anyhow, this man, the owner of the French Line, he was just so surprised that it really was a child, he says, 'Well,' he says, 'any time that you're going to Europe, you go as my guest. Free, all the way.'"

"Did you take him up on it?"

"No, we didn't book Europe back then."

"When did he become the second highest paid child performer?"

"Well, he got seven hundred and fifty dollars a week in Australia, which was the highest paid single that ever went there, at that time. And when we came back from Australia, we went right to work, and it just kept growing. It went up to a thousand a week before very long. Back in the twenties, that was very big money."

I couldn't help laughing at that, the way he tossed it off, almost parenthetically, and then he laughed, too. I was grateful for the mood, because we had gotten to a point in the conversation when I had to ask some difficult questions, and I'd been worried about how to do it. I didn't really want to ask them, because I cared about Bob, and I was afraid I might hurt his feelings. I had seriously considered not asking them at all, and going to someone else for confirmation of what I suspected, but I knew that wouldn't be any good. I decided to ask a few oblique questions, to watch his reactions with extreme care, and to stop instantly if I sensed that it was going to be painful.

When we stopped laughing, there was a pause, and he looked at me and smiled a bit stiffly, as if he knew what was coming and understood that I had to do it. I remember hearing music from a portable radio somewhere nearby and the sound of distant voices.

"Buddy retired from vaudeville when he was about fourteen?"

"About fourteen, somewhere in there."

"And you came back to Brooklyn to live, to settle down?"

"That's right."

"What was done to continue his education?"

"His education?"

I watched his eyes carefully. "Did he try to go to school again?"

He squinted at the sea. "No. We had a teacher, a tutor, that I paid so much a week."

"Yes, he'd been taking the correspondence courses—"

"Oh, yeah, sure, that's—"

"—and those were past, but I wondered why, at fourteen, he didn't start in a regular school? Because he wasn't working then."

He hesitated, still looking at the sea. "We had fighting to do then, fighting to get booking. He was neither child nor grownup. And it was tough getting work. Because he outgrew the baby business. And he wasn't old enough to be on his own and travel on his own."

"He didn't join Joe Marsala's band until nineteen thirty-eight, when he was twenty, twenty-one. That was the first regular job he was offered as a jazz drummer. It must've been a very rough period between fourteen and twenty-one."

He blinked in the glare. "It was rough. We had a rough period."

I took a deep breath, spoke softly. "In all those years—six, seven years—why didn't he go to school?"

He continued to gaze at the sea, and I was about to change the subject, when he smiled, a gentle smile, as if he had seen an old friend, and his voice was soft and warm. "When Buddy was fourteen, we were practically broke. We were living at a place called the Hotel America on Forty-seventh Street. That was in nineteen thirty-one, and things were very bad. I remember, there were these kids from Pittsburgh, a set band, and they were stranded. They were on the breadline and we took them in, we took them to this Hotel America with us. And, oh, were we broke. And they were broke. And we had the one room. And they used to come up, and

they hadn't eaten, and I used to get a few bucks and go over to—
Eighth or Ninth Avenue. They had markets below the West Side
Highway. They had markets on the ground there—pushcarts, you
know? And I used to buy eggs, about ten or twelve cents a dozen,
and a loaf of bread." He laughed quietly to himself. "Go back to
the hotel. We had a one-burner thing, you know? And I used to fry
eggs on there and feed the whole bunch, and ourselves as well.
No, we had rough times and good times, you know. As he got
older, we kept using up what we had, and pretty soon we had
nothing left. But that was all—that was all a long time ago, when
we were very young and very happy."

9

FRIDAY, september 13, 1974, the front page of *The New York Times* had lead articles announcing that President Ford did not intend to pardon any of the Watergate defendants before trial, as he had pardoned Nixon on September 8, and that Ethiopia's Emperor, Haile Selassie, had been deposed by the military after having ruled for fifty-eight years. The sports pages told how the Yankees shut out the Orioles in Baltimore and were leading the American League's Eastern Division by two and one-half games, with eighteen to go, and how *Courageous* had defeated Australia's *Southern Cross* for the second straight time in the America's Cup mismatch. And, in the entertainment section, there was a review titled "One Mel Swoop," by Steven R. Weisman, which began:

> This may be Friday the 13th, but don't let that stop you from celebrating the autumnal rites in New York that are marked by the beginning of the nightclub season. The city's elegant hotels are opening with fresh acts, in some cases, and the appearance of old favorites, in others.
>
> At the St. Regis-Sheraton, Fifth Avenue and 55th Street, Mel Tormé has opened the new season at the Maisonette for the third year in a row. He's a favorite over there because of his bantering manner and the pleasure he takes in singing to the big sounds of the orchestra, or to the sparse but sweet sounds of his own ukulele...

That evening, Mel Tormé didn't play the ukulele, but when I entered the Maisonette Room at 7:45 with Marie, Buddy, Sandi, and Stanley, Mel's drums had a place of honor on the dance floor next to the stage. It was a complete Slingerland set, exactly the same as Buddy's, even to the white marine pearl of the frames, except for his initials, "MT" on the bass drum, in a shield, against two vertical stripes.

Buddy smiled and shook his head when he saw the set. "One thing about Mel," he told me, "the man's got guts."

We were given the best table in the room, front and center, at the edge of the dance floor. Virtually every table was occupied, and waiters moved around silently on the thick carpeting, serving dinner before the first show. I remember the soft lighting and the walls lined with bookcases and oil paintings, and how stunning Marie looked in a black sequined hat, silk shirt, and black St. Laurent velveteen pantsuit that enhanced her slim figure. Buddy, on her right, looked smart in a blue blazer, blue shirt, ascot, and glasses, kept glancing at her with obvious pride, and seemed very "up," partly because of the extremely effective "Topic A" newsfilm that had been shown on NBC just about an hour before. Sharon Sopher, the producer, had not used the interview recorded in his dressing room, but the voice-over narration by Scott Osborne was superbly written and delivered, and the footage included a record store with the best jazz collection in New York, where Buddy was listed as one of the most popular artists of the year; a wide range of scenes at the club, including short interviews with members of the audience and, finally, scenes from the recording session, with a section of fast cuts synchronized to the music itself, and unusually lively shots of Buddy, Lionel Hampton, Teddy Wilson, Zoot Sims, and George Duvivier, all at work and having a ball together, along with producer Sonny Lester, president of Groove Merchant, who was dancing with Marie and Cathy in the control room.

We had drinks and ordered dinner. Paul Burke, the actor, was supposed to join us with his date, but they were very late. Marie was concerned about me because I didn't have a date, but I assured her that I didn't mind. My wife, Verity, an executive with Pan Am, was off again on one of her frequent business trips, this time to Honolulu, Tokyo, Seoul, Hong Kong, Bangkok, Singapore, and Saigon. She was gone for many weeks at a time that summer and autumn, and it wasn't half as glamorous as it sounded; she worked seven days a week and the schedule was usually hectic beyond belief, but she loved it.

As we were finishing our appetizers, Paul Burke finally arrived with his attractive date, Cathy Kelly, and although I had never met him or even seen him in person, I knew his face, voice, and mannerisms quite well. He'd starred on the television series *Naked City* and *Twelve O'clock High* for many years and appeared in numerous feature films, and Stanley told me he was in town to appear in *Police Woman* and to do several television commercials for Radio Shack. Paul was in his late forties that year and had been a close friend of Stanley's for about eighteen years. Born in New Orleans, he was a jazz aficionado, an amateur drummer, and a long-time fan of Buddy's.

We had a pleasant dinner and the show started at almost exactly nine, with Al Porcino's fifteen-member orchestra launching into its theme, *Jubilee*. I kept my eyes on Porcino, who was generally regarded as one of the finest lead-trumpet players; he had traveled and recorded with virtually all of the greats and, several years ago, with Buddy's big band. Jazz critic Leonard Feather had written that Buddy's band marched with "power and togetherness" under Porcino, "a trumpet player who could safely lead a brass section through a brush fire." He proved it that night.

The orchestra played several selections and nobody introduced Mel Tormé—he just appeared. The spotlight swung to the left corner of the room near the stage, and he walked onto the dance floor with polished confidence in a well-tailored tuxedo, and received immediate and heavy applause. The hair had thinned and he was no longer hollow-cheeked but the eyes and smile and attitude were remarkably unchanged over the years, and his voice still had the same relaxed, mellow quality as he took the microphone and introduced his drummer, Butch Miles. Mel was celebrating his forty-ninth birthday that evening, a fact that he announced softly but proudly, and I must say I liked that. Everyone in the audience liked the way he did that.

Then he was into his act: "One thing, one thing I have to tell you, that what I just did, walking on this stage, is a calculated risk." Laughter. "No, no, I'll tell you why. Because, you realize what happens? I walk out, I start to look around at the people, and I see—thank *God!*—a nice large area of recognition. But, occasionally, as I look at ringside, I see a few people looking up at me, and I *know* what's going on in their minds—they're going, 'Who the hell is *that?*' Now, that's because I come on stage totally unannounced. Which is, as I say, a terrible risk. No matter how long you've been in the business, there's always going to be *some*body that doesn't know you. So, for anybody here that doesn't know me, may I please introduce myself: Good evening, my name is Steve Lawrence." Loud laughter. "My wife, Edie *Tormé*, will be out in a minute, folks, but first—" The laughter was loud and genuine, with scattered applause, and then he was into his first song, *Taking a Chance on Love*, followed by five other favorites. The familiar voice was as good, if not better, than I had ever heard it, with more nuances, and, when the occasion demanded, he summoned a deep and full resonance that I had never realized he had. His own arrangement of a Gershwin melody was a high point of the show and he accompanied himself at the piano.

Finally, it was time to introduce Buddy, and he did it with considerable pleasure: "I don't know if you looked at the news tonight, but there was a big story on NBC News, around the ten-to-seven mark, about the resurgence of jazz and how popular it's becoming; tremendous upsurge of sales in jazz records. And they did a marvelous piece tonight, ladies and gentlemen, on my favorite place in this town—other than the Maisonette—and that's Buddy's Place over on—" he turned, glanced at Butch Miles up on stage—"Second, right?"

"Right."

"Second Avenue?"

"Right."

He turned back. "Sixty-first and Second. The reason it's called Buddy's Place is that the world's greatest drummer owns the joint and plays there intermittently. He happens to be there right now, except that he's not really there right now, he's in our midst tonight. And I'm very pleased and flattered that my friend of over thirty years came in to say hello this evening, which happens to be, as I said, my birthday. I'd very much like to have you meet—very simply, because anything else is superfluous—the world's greatest drummer, and I mean for all time: Mr. Buddy Rich."

Buddy stood up, nodded to the applause, then sat down and called out, "Sixty-*fourth* Street," but the ovation hadn't ended and hardly anyone heard him.

"What?" Mel asked.

"It's on Sixty-*fourth* Street."

The whole room broke up with laughter, and Mel was a bit flustered, laughing himself, saying, "Sixty-*fourth*? I'm sorry, Sixty-fourth and Second," but the way he said it got even more laughter. When he regained his composure, he added, "Well, I was there during the telethon, I was a little *tired*, you know?"

After introducing Paul Burke, whom he hadn't expected, Mel walked to his drums, smiled broadly, and told the crowd: "When you see what I'm about to attempt, with Buddy Rich in the room, you're really going to see an example of guts football—look out!" He grabbed the sticks, gave the downbeat, and the orchestra blasted into *Fascinatin' Rhythm*, with Mel not only going wild on the drums, but singing the lyrics.

At 10:15, the maitre d' rolled out a huge white birthday cake and presented it on behalf of the hotel. Buddy had to leave then, because he was already late for his own show at the club. Stanley went with him.

I stayed with Marie, Sandi, Paul, and Cathy Kelly. Mel was presented with a large plaque from the Muscular Dystrophy Association of America for his work on the recently completed telethon, which set an all-time record, $16 million in contributions. He had set something of a record himself by being the only performer on the telethon, live, on both sides of the continent, starting at the Sahara in Las Vegas, then flying to New York to co-host with Jerry Lewis.

A few minutes after the show ended, Mel's manager, Gary Stevens, came to our table and told us that Mel would cut his second show to forty-five minutes and try to catch Buddy's last show at 1:15.

Outside, it was raining again, as was the case most of the day, and we waited under the canopy as the doorman whistled for taxis. Sandi got in the first one with Paul and Cathy; Marie and I took the next one. Traffic was heavy and horns were blowing all over.

We had to turn left at Fifth Avenue because it was one-way, south, then left again at Fifty-fourth, and left at Madison, heading uptown. Marie sat back quietly and I remember how the brim of her hat, turned down, cast a shadow over her eyes, and how the soft reflections of headlights moved across the lower part of her face.

"Quite a show," I said.

She nodded. "Mel's a very talented man, always has been. God, seeing him tonight, it brought back so many memories. They've been friends since—well, nineteen forty-five, at least, back in the Dorsey years. That was long before I'd even met Buddy." She looked out at the rain.

"How did you actually meet Buddy?"

"Through Gene Krupa."

"Where was it, what happened?"

Marie smiled, continued to look out the window. "They had both come out to Los Angeles to do Jazz at the Philharmonic, they were both working it together. Gene was an old boyfriend of mine and I hadn't seen him for a while, and he evidently had been telling Buddy all about me on their trip out to California. So when Gene got to the coast, he called; he asked me to have dinner with them. It was like a very ticklish thing, because I'd been dating him for about seven years, off and on, and he was married. I met him on that first film I'd worked in, *George White's Scandals*, and, at that time, he wasn't married."

"Was he playing in the film?"

"Yeah, the Gene Krupa Orchestra was in it, with Joan Davis and Jack Haley and Ethel Smith and Betty Jane Greer, and then all the kids that were under contract. Anyhow, I met Gene and this attraction started. And I was married but the marriage wasn't working out. So, when I got a divorce, I got in touch with him. But, in the meantime, I'd gone to South America on a junket and I was gone about three months, and while I was in South America he had remarried his first wife. But I didn't know that and when I got back to New York I picked up a paper and I found out he was playing at a place called the Aquarium. And I went down there, and it was so marvelous to see him, and we went out afterwards and had a drink, and then he told me he had remarried his first wife. It was very tragic, because I really, really liked him. And I would still see him. His marriage wasn't working out. It hadn't worked out the first time, and it wasn't working out any better the second time. So, off and on, I saw Gene for about seven years. That would be just before I married Buddy. Like, Gene was really a big hangup in my life, and that prevented me from doing a lot in the movies, because whenever he'd pick up the phone and say, 'I'm on the road, come and join me,' I did it. And I got the reputation around town of not being very dependable. It was a village, you know, Hollywood was a village. And a couple of times I had signed to do a film, had made a commitment, and Gene would call and I'd take off. So, anyhow, it lasted seven years, because Gene kept telling me he was going to leave his wife, that he really wanted me. And I believed him. And he didn't leave her. So, finally, I put my foot down and I said, 'This is it. The next time I see you, you're going to be single. And don't call me any more.' And it had been about a year and a half since I'd heard from him, when he came out to the coast with Buddy. And I was going with Hal March. Do you remember Hal March?"

"Oh, yes, very well."

She looked at me then and her voice became more animated, with just a hint of vivaciousness, like Cathy's. "Well, Hal was fantastic and I really had a good time with him. I wasn't in love with him, but it was like I was settling. I wanted to get married. So, Gene called, and I told Hal about it, and he says, 'Well, look, have dinner with him and see how you feel.' Hal says, 'Because if you still feel that way about him, maybe we shouldn't get married.' I went to dinner with Gene and I still felt the same way, but I wasn't going to tell Hal that, because Gene wasn't about to leave Ethel. Again, we had dinner at LaRue's, and Gene told me he had become very friendly with Buddy on his last tour. And he says, 'Now, after dinner, I want you to come out to the concert at Long Beach.' And he says, 'In fact, Buddy's going to pick us up and we'll drive to the concert with him.' So, we finished our dinner, and at the designated time we're standing out in front of LaRue's, and Buddy drives up in his Cadillac with his valet. And Gene and I get in the back seat. And my first impression of Buddy was, 'My God, he's so much younger than I thought he was,' because he'd been around such a long time. And I'd never, ever, seen him before. I'd only heard a lot of stories about him through Gene."

"This was in the early fifties?"

"Oh, yes, this was around nineteen fifty-one, fifty-two." She glanced out the window again and the reflection of the rain moved down her face in soft patterns. "So we get in the back and Gene and I talk all the way to Long Beach, and Buddy told me later that he was watching me through the rear-view mirror, but I didn't know it. And I thought, 'He's kind of cute, he looks like a college kid,' and that was it. Now, we get to Long Beach and I start to get out of the car, but there was like a little black duffel bag that was behind Buddy's seat, and I was sitting behind Buddy. And when he pulled back the seat to let me out, he saw the bag and he shouted at the valet: 'How come that was left there! It must've been very uncomfortable for Marie! Why didn't you put it—!' And I thought, 'Hmmm.' I didn't like the flare-up of temper, but it made me feel kind of good that he'd been that considerate of me, so concerned. So, he and his valet walk on up ahead of us, going to the auditorium, and Gene and I are just kind of strolling, and I said to him—you know, I didn't mean it, because I just thought there was no contest, that Gene was the better drummer—and I said to Gene, we're arm and arm, and I said, 'Tell me, which one's the better drummer?'"

We had just stopped for a traffic light and she seemed lost in her thoughts, frowning, shaking her head slightly, as if to deny the memory. I can remember the soft, rhythmic sound of the windshield wipers in the semidarkness.

"Why'd he say?" I asked softly

"He drew himself up, and then I realized maybe something was wrong, maybe Gene wasn't actually the better drummer, because of his reaction. And he says, 'Well, suppose I let you be the judge.' So I stood in the wings and I watched the show. Buddy's group came out and did their spot, then Gene's group came out and did their spot. No, I'm sorry, Gene came out first and did his spot, and I'd seen him play many, many times, of course. He finished up with the spotlight on the drum, you know, and the huge shadow on the wall in back, with the hair flying and the sticks flying. Okay, I'd been used to seeing that; it was very good."

She waited a moment, until the light changed and we started again, then looked at me. "Then Buddy came out. And Buddy just—tore it up. It was like—*unbelievable.* I couldn't *believe* what I was seeing. And if I could only remember names—the jazz trumpet player who was in Gene's group, they called him 'Little Jazz,' what's his name? He used to be in Gene's big band, he sang with Anita O'Day, *Let Me Off Uptown,* what's his name?"

I thought about it. "Roy Eldridge?"

"Roy Eldridge, right. Now, when Buddy's group was on, Gene went upstairs to his dressing room, he didn't come around and stand with me. Roy Eldridge came and stood with me. And he was talking to me about Buddy, and he says, "Yeah, he's good,' he says, 'but he doesn't dress like Gene, he doesn't have that style, like with the backdrop.' And I realized for the first time what he was doing. He knew that Buddy was better, and he knew that I wasn't going to be able to tell that Buddy was better, and maybe Gene had sent him down to talk to me. I don't know how it was, but it was like I'd formed my opinion then, and up to that point, you know, Krupa was the greatest drummer in the world."

"Because you'd never actually seen Buddy play."

"Right. So it was very smart of the producer to pit the two together, and that was the end of the show, where they would both come out on stage and do their 'Battle of the Drums,' Gene and Buddy. And when they did it that night, it was obvious who was the best; it was obvious to everybody. And when I went upstairs to the dressing room after the concert, Gene started drinking in the dressing room—he'd started drinking even before I got up there—and I knew he was disturbed about it. Evidently, I was kind of important to him, and what I thought about his ability as a musician was important to him. So, he says, 'Well, what'd you think? Who's the better drummer?' And I said—I lied and I said—'You are, of course.' I mean, I just had to. Because I could see that it was such a touchy spot. Then I came down out of the dressing room, while Gene changed his clothes. And I was standing in like the entrance to the place, and there was an outside telephone there, and Buddy was on the telephone *screaming* at somebody. And I just stood there. And the whole drift of the conversation was, it had to do with some girl, and he was screaming: 'What do you *mean* you did that! How *could* you, how *dare* you! Okay, that's *all*, that's *it*!' And I thought, 'Hmmm, isn't he interesting.'"

She laughed like a little girl and I had to laugh.

"Then, coming back from Long Beach, Buddy's cousin, Jackie, rode back with us, and we got back to the place Gene had left his car, in Hollywood. And it had all been prearranged—Buddy got Gene very busy on the car and, on the side that I got out of, cousin Jackie came over to me and he says, 'Hey, Buddy really digs you, he'd like to have your telephone number.' And I had heard that Buddy was married. And that was *it* with married men for me, you know, the thing with Gene—God, much too long. I said, 'I hear he's married.' He says, 'That's not true.' I said, 'Well, it's a very strong rumor.' He says, 'No, he's been living with some chick for seven years, but he's not married to her.' And he says, 'They're not together any more.' So I said, 'Well, okay, you know, I'll give him my number. I don't know if I'll go out with him, but he can have my number.' So I gave it to Jackie, and Buddy called bright and early the next day."

I laughed softly. "The next morning?"

"Yeah! And he says, 'Look,' he says, 'I haven't been in California for years. Most of the girls I knew out here are married, or they've moved away and I've lost contact.' And he says, 'Do you know any attractive girls?'"

"Oh, no, not *that* number."

"Oh, yes. So I said, 'Yes, I have one extremely attractive girl-friend that you'd probably like a lot.' And I said, 'I'll call her and I'll find out if it's all right to give out her number.' So he says, 'What does she look like?' And I described her, I said, 'She's tall and she's brunette and she's gorgeous.' And he says—in this little tiny voice—he says, 'But I like blondes.' And there was the opener, you know: 'Will you have dinner with me?' 'I don't like to go out with married men.' 'But I'm *not* married.' You know, the whole thing, all over again. So I said, 'Well, look, I don't really feel that I should accept a date with you under the circumstances, because you and Gene are working together, and it just isn't cool. And I wouldn't hurt Gene for anything in the world, nor would I embarrass him. You know, I really don't owe him anything, but I feel that's the way I'd like it to be.' So he says, 'Will you have dinner with me if it's all right with Gene?' He was persistent. So I said, 'Okay, I expect to hear from Gene later this afternoon and I'll ask him.' And Gene called me and I said, 'Buddy wanted my telephone number last night and I gave it to him. He's asked me to go to dinner.' I said, 'How do you feel about that?' Silence. And then he says, 'Look, he's a nice guy, he really is nice.' And he says, 'I can't tell you not to go.' So I said, 'Okay.' Just before I hung up, he says, 'Don't fall in love with him.' That was it. And then Buddy and I went to dinner that night."

We stopped for another traffic light at Madison and Sixty-fourth, and the driver flicked on his directional signal to turn right. It made a rapid clicking in counterpoint to the windshield wipers.

"Do you remember where you went?" I asked.

"We had dinner at a place called Tail O' the Cock. It used to be on La Cienega, I think it's still there. And I had my double martini before dinner, and Buddy, who I didn't know was a *non*-drinker, ordered a double martini. And we sat and we talked and we talked and we *talked* and we talked. And I ordered another double martini and *he* ordered another double martini. And, all of a sudden, I realized that he was drunk. You know? I mean, he was feeling pretty good. And then we ordered dinner. And I guess the excitement of being together, neither one of us ate very much; we kept talking and drinking. And we wound up at a place to hear a girl named Kitty White, a place in Beverly Hills called—"

She paused, trying hard to remember. The light changed and we headed east on Sixty-fourth in fairly heavy traffic.

"I can't think of it," she said finally. It was a very 'in' place to go at the time and it's no longer in existence. And we sat there and we listened to her sing." She gestured with her hands: "She was over there, and our table was facing this way, because it was extremely crowded, and I was turned, watching Kitty. Buddy couldn't figure it out—he was so looped, he couldn't figure out where the music was coming from, and he was staring straight *ahead*." She laughed, remembering, seeing it clearly. "And I had a friend who was standing at the bar, and he caught this whole thing; and finally, when Kitty took an intermission, he leaned over to me—there was like a slatted partition—and he leaned over, we were in this little booth, and he leaned over and tapped my shoulder and I turned around. And he whispers, 'Marie, are you all right? Do you need some help?'" She laughed again, very softly. "And I said, 'I'm fine, Ralph, I'm okay!' He says, 'All right,' goes away. So we get up, somehow, I don't know how Buddy made it out of the club—I wish I could remember the name of the place—and I had to drive the Caddy to my apartment, because he couldn't drive. And we stood out in front and he wanted to kiss me goodnight, and so I kissed him. And he started to grab me and I pulled his hand away. And that impressed him a *lot*, he said later. That impressed him a *lot*. I don't know what he thought. So, that night, he asked me to marry him."

"My God."

She nodded. "And I told him, I said, 'You're drunk.' But it scared the shit out of me. I said, 'You're drunk and you don't know what you're saying and you don't know anything about me.'"

"This is right out in front of your place?"

She nodded again, narrowed her eyes to the window; lights moved across her profile. "And he says, 'I know everything about you that I need to know.' I guess from what Gene had told him. I said, 'Well, you'd better go home and sober up.' And so he called me the next morning, he woke me up. And I said, 'Hello.' And he says, 'Will you marry me?' And I really got scared, you know, it was like, it was weird. And he was leaving—Jazz at the Philharmonic was going to Honolulu, that was the next concert. And he asked me to go. And, because of Gene, I wouldn't go. And he called me from Honolulu and asked me to come over. I said, 'No, I can't do that.' So I met him at the airport when they came back, and we drove to Palm Springs. And we made it then. It was like, he wanted to get married and that was it. And he flew to

New York, and it broke in the papers that we were going to be married, and poor Hal March didn't know what happened to *him*. And Gene called me—when he read it in the columns, he called me out in California. And he was drunk. And he says, 'What's this that I'm reading about?' He says, 'Is it true?' I said, 'Well, Buddy *has* asked me to marry him.' He says, 'Are you going to?' I said, 'I don't know, I really haven't decided yet.' And he says, 'You're going to wind up worse than you are now, if you do.' I said, 'Gene, that sounds like sour grapes. You know, like, you don't want me, but you don't want anybody else to have me.' And we hung up and that was it. Later on, after Buddy and I were married for a while, Gene apologized for saying that."

All along Sixty-fourth Street, traffic was jammed bumper-to-bumper in the rain and horns were blowing. Marie started laughing at something and continued laughing as she spoke.

"Then I flew to New York to be married and Buddy met me at the airport. And, like, I was moving here, so I had a lot of luggage and a lot of hand-luggage, and this nice guy that was sitting next to me on the plane helped me with some of my hand-luggage. And Buddy saw us walking down the ramp together and talking—"

I laughed then, anticipating her, picturing it.

"Right? And we got to Buddy, you know, and I didn't know the guy's name or anything, so I didn't introduce him, I just thanked him very much and he put my things down and left. And Buddy's *pouting*, and I don't know, I hadn't seen this side of him directed at *me*, so I don't know what's wrong. We walk to the car, we wait for my luggage, and he's not talking to me. Finally, the porter loads the car and we're driving into Manhattan and he finally blasts me—he thought I was with that guy. So it was just one bad scene after the other. And, after a few weeks, neither of us wanted to get married. And yet, my family thought I was all set to get married, my friends thought we were all set, because I'd flown here to be married. And each day we'd have another fight, and we never got down to the justice of the peace to get a license. And I was in New York about—I guess it was about three or four months, living with him, and now he decides that he's going to join Harry James's band, he's going to go to California and join them out there. And I had very mixed emotions about going out there with him, because all my friends were out there, and we weren't married. So we went out there and we checked into the Beverly Hills Hotel as 'Mr. and Mrs.'"

In the pause, she touched her lips, then tapped her fingers against her lips. "I guess it was longer, I guess we were on the East Coast longer than three or four months, because we actually lived together six months before we were married. Anyway, he played the Palladium about a month with Harry and then they were going on tour, and their first one-nighter was Yuma, Arizona. And Buddy was—'See you later, kid,' you know? Like, he was going to leave his car with me and everything and he just figured I'd hang around and wait. And I said, 'You can't *do* that to me.' He says, 'What do you *mean*?' I said, 'Everybody thinks we're *married*!' So I begged to go on tour with him and he finally gave in. And as we were driving to Yuma, Arizona, here were all these signs, and they're saying—you know, they're marriage places—'Married Immediately, No Waiting, No Tests,' like, on each side of the road. And I'm looking at all these signs, and I'm looking at Buddy, and he's like this—" She grabbed an imaginary steering wheel and stared fixedly ahead, eyes wide, laughing. "He's driving the Cadillac—was it a Jag or a Cadillac? I think he had the Jag that time. Yeah, because he picked up a new Jag in New York and drove it cross-country. Driving the Jag like this, and he's not looking, and, as we pull into the main part of town, there's like a little park, a little circle, and then the hotel where the band was staying was there, and the band bus was parked out front, and they were unloading, and here's a justice of the peace on this side of the road, in a little curve-around, you know?"

She hesitated, glanced at me, and when she continued, her voice rose and fell in spurts, almost musically, full of excitement and laughter, as if the memory had quickened something deep inside that had not been called to consciousness for many years.

"So, he starts to pull up by the bus, and he slows down by the justice of the peace, and he stops the car and he says, 'All *right*, go in and find out what you have to *do*!' And I went *flying*, you know? And then—oh, it was terrible, I couldn't get my clothes off the bus? And I was married in the slacks that I traveled in? But I figured, I'd better do it now, you know, I'd better not wait till I get my clothes off the bus, because he might not ask me again. And Harry James was Buddy's best man, and Sal Monte, the manager of the band, was my matron of honor! And we had a justice of the peace that had a very decided British accent, and it was just—it was just so weird for that part of the country, that Harry and Buddy and Sal were cracking up all through the ceremony, and I was *crying*, because they were laughing all the way through my marriage ceremony! And that's the way we were married. That was it. April twenty-first, nineteen fifty-three, that made me an honest woman. And, you know, he always says to me, like, 'You know, I really didn't want to get *married*!' And I forced it—I did."

"Did you go on any honeymoon of any kind?"

"No. We never had one, really."

There was a pause. We listened to the windshield wipers.

"We should take one," she said, almost in a whisper.

"Yes, you should."

Then the smile again, remembering. "It was just—it was really weird, living together for six months, and then we were married April twenty-first, and Cathy was born the following year, May eleventh. So it was like I was being—I was protected for some reason, and as soon as we got married—well, about four months later, in August, I got pregnant."

"Where were you living then?"

She turned to the window again and her voice became very soft, almost lyrical. "We lived in California all the time I was pregnant, and, looking back, I suppose that was one of the happiest times of our lives. Cathy changed everything in our lives, and Buddy changed remarkably, almost from the day she was born. He absolutely adores her, and I do, too. Without any question, Cathy is one of the big reasons why our marriage lasted all these years, while most of our friends have long since been divorced. And now, she'll be twenty-one next year, and she's bound to move out, sooner or later, and make her own life. We don't want to lose her, of course, it's going to hurt terribly, but Buddy knows as well as I do that it's going to happen soon. And when it does, and we're alone again, I wonder, I seriously wonder—what will happen to us?"

IO

ON SEPTEMBER 15, 1974, Buddy and I had breakfast in the coffee shop of the Sheraton-Universal Hotel in North Hollywood. We sat at a table in the sun near the pool and he kept laughing about the previous night. We had been watching television in the room, after the flight from New York, and I started to fall asleep during *Police Story*. I asked him to be sure and wake me for *The Tonight Show* at 11:30 and he agreed. But I was so fast asleep by show time (2:30 New York time), and snoring, he decided not to wake me—a decision he later regretted.

"You're unbelievable, man," he told me, laughing. "You snore so loud, it's absolutely *unbelievable*. Like, you're not *human*. The *windows* shook. The *beds* shook. I went in the bathroom, the *mirrors* shook. I went out in the hall, closed the door, the *door* shook like it was coming off its hinges. It was weird, I thought I was having a nightmare. By the time Johnny Carson came on, I had to start turning up the volume, because you seemed to be getting even louder. Finally, I get up, go over to your bed, turn you on your other side, you know, thought that'd help. No way. Snored *louder*. I tried to wake you up—I yelled, *'Hey, John!'* Nothing." He cupped his hands, laughing. "Then I yelled right into your ear: *'Hey, man, shut up!'* Nothing. Sounded like a pig having an orgasm. Then I grabbed you and *shook* you. Nothing. I thought, 'The cat's not *human*.' I mean, I used to think Sinatra was bad. He used to sit up in bed, late at night, and clip his fingernails slowly. Like, click, click, click, click, you know, middle of the night, used to drive me up the wall. Last night, it was so bad, I *apologized* to Frank, out loud. Said, 'Frank, I take it all back, man, I'm sorry, I didn't know what a *prince* you were! Forgive me, man, *wherever* you are!'"

I sat back and laughed hard. The thought occurred to me that if you gave him half a chance he could go on like that indefinitely, off in a world of his own.

"Like, how does you *wife* stand it?" he asked. "How does Verity cope with it?"

"Turns on the air conditioner. Full blast."

"Yeah? What about in winter?"

"She has a special sleep machine."

That broke him up. "She has a—she has a *what*?"

"A sleep machine, called 'Sleep Sound.' Bought it in Hammacher Schlemmer, they have several models. Very big seller."

"What the hell does it *do*?"

"Makes a sound like rushing air, like an air conditioner. Other models, you can have the sound of the sea, wind, rain—"

"Man, you'd need one that sounds like a nuclear *explosion*!"

Buddy was to appear on *The Tonight Show* that evening and I remember we talked about Johnny Carson at some length: the way he changed the show when he replaced Jack Paar in 1962; the reasons why competing talk-shows had never dislodged him from the top spot in the ratings; how humor had changed in the show's twelve-year history. Back in July, *TV Guide* had published a cover story titled, *Whe-e-e-e-ere's Johnny?* in which the writer insisted that Carson had a "well-known, near-pathological aversion to interviews," and I asked Buddy about that.

"Yeah, I read it, too," he said.

"You think there's any truth to it?"

He thought about it. "I know he has an aversion to being misquoted, like everybody else. I know he has an aversion to having his statements taken out of context and twisted around. A lot of writers are looking for sensationalism, and he avoids them, because he hates that whole scene. Off the set, he's a quiet, private guy, and he expects people to respect that privacy, that's all. God knows, he's earned that right. There's nothing 'pathological' about that." He lit a cigarette, inhaled deeply. "I can prove it to you. I'll give him a call, see if he's free, try to set up a short interview for you this afternoon."

The interview was scheduled for two o'clock and a studio limo picked us up at 1:30. It was a short, pleasant drive to Universal City Studios. We drove through the guarded front gate, then on through the gate marked "Artists' Entrance." Buddy had been there so many times, he didn't need to be shown through the labyrinth of corridors, offices, and sets. His dressing room was just off the *Tonight* set, with his name on the door and a caricature of his face.

We walked upstairs to Carson's office. His attractive blond secretary sat at a desk in the waiting room, to the left of the door; behind her, the door to the actual office was wide open, but I couldn't see anybody. The waiting room was fairly large, thickly carpeted, and the walls and shelves held hundreds of photographs and memorabilia.

The girl smiled at Buddy, then at me. "You must be Mr. Minahan."

"That's right."

She turned to her left, called into the office: "Mr. Minahan is here with Mr. Rich."

Carson's familiar voice called back: "I'll see Mr. Minahan, but I'm *out* to Mr. Rich. Tell him I'm out of town, tell him I'm out of the country—anything."

There was laughter as she escorted us in. Buddy introduced us, we shook hands, then Buddy and Johnny were into a bear hug, laughing.

Carson looked at the bandage on Buddy's left hand. "What the—what the hell's that thing on your *hand*?"

"Oh, man, it's—"

"The same *finger*! Christ, it's the same finger as *last* year!"

"Almost to the day."

"Not tennis again, not—"

"No, no, karate this time, blocked a kick."

Johnny turned, gave me one of his famed blank looks. "Greatest drummer in the world. Million-dollar hands. Blocks karate kicks with his fingers." He took a deep breath, raised his eyebrows. "Ho-kay."

Buddy left the office laughing and closed the door. Johnny shook his head, laughed softly, indicated a chair near his "desk," which was actually a long coffee table, piled with papers, then sat behind it. There was an open rectangular window behind him, throwing bright sunlight on the handsome furniture. He looked relaxed in a white sport shirt with blue designs, dark trousers, white sneakers, no socks. His face seemed more red than tan, as if he had just come in from several hours in the strong sun.

"Do you mind if I use a tape recorder?"

He leaned back on the couch, hands behind his head. "Actually, I'd rather you didn't use it, if you don't mind."

"Not at all." I reached to my left, placed the tape recorder on a corner table.

He handed me a legal-sized pad of tan-colored paper, lined, with his name in the upper right-hand corner. "You can take all the notes you want. It's just that writers who've used tape have really come up with some—this last guy, from *TV Guide*, wow!"

"The cover story, yes, I read it."

"I mean, he was dragging up things from thirty years ago."

"I know."

"Who needs it? That's why—I've just decided not to give interviews any more, that's all. I just won't give them."

"This is just about Buddy. You and Buddy."

"Right, this is different, I don't mind this."

I took a pencil from the holder on the table. "You've known Buddy—what, twenty years now?"

He lit a cigarette, sat back. "I think—at least that long, yes."

"Can you remember, approximately, when you first met him?"

He looked away, smiled warmly. "Actually, I remember it quite well. It was at a place called Larry Potter's Supper Club out here. This was about nineteen fifty, fifty-one, somewhere in there. He had an act called 'That's Rich.' I remember it because it *has* to be the worst act I ever saw in my life. It was just absolutely awful. A couple of things stand out clearly. About five years ago, in Vegas, I saw him come in one of the hotels and listen to some band play the last few minutes of *West Side Story*, then go up and play it himself like it was never played before. And there was a place we used to go to called The Chez, in Hollywood; they got together about twenty, twenty-five drummers for a session one time. When Buddy played *West Side Story*, he went all-out, gave it everything, telling his story, and it was such a tour de force, so utterly brilliant and inspired, that a lot of them were actually crying. I remember Sperling, particularly, crying hard. Now that's—that's something else. When you see professionals moved that much. I don't think anyone who was there will ever forget that."

"If you had to describe who Buddy Rich is, in just a few words, how would you put it?"

He hesitated for just a moment, then leaned forward. "I'd say he's a combination of Billy Graham and Attila the Hun."

We both laughed out loud, Carson with his familiar all-out laugh, and I remember his eyes filled, laughing, and he put his hand up to wipe them.

"Why do you think he adopts the 'tough guy' attitude?" I asked.

"Well, I just think it evolved gradually, I don't think it was a conscious thing. I remember in the early forties, before he went into service, he never even swore in public. That was before we actually met, but we had mutual friends, of course, and they all verify the fact. I think the service changed him. I mean, it's his image now, the heavy, the tough guy, we always fool around with it on the show. We throw lines with that intention, to reinforce the image. But he's basically a very shy man. Last Saturday, we did a rerun of the show he did about a year ago, when his daughter Cathy was on—"

"Yes, I saw that."

"You see that? And it was her first time on the show. I think it was her first network appearance, and she sang a song, I can't remember—"

"*What Will They Say?*"

"That's right, of course, that was it. And Buddy's sitting next to me, watching her sing, and—I swear to God—he was crying like a baby. Tears streaming down his cheeks. If the audience could've seen him, they simply wouldn't have believed it. Would've blown his whole image. Have you—I suppose you've seen him like that?"

"Once in a while, yes. He's very guarded about things like that."

"I remember something he did one time, it really got to me." He stood up, motioned for me to stand. "We were in New York, I think, and he came up to me like this..." He stood next to me, looked away, pretended to put something in the left front pocket of my trousers. "He said, 'Here's something for you,' or mumbled something to that effect, and walked away quickly—he was gone in a flash. Well, it was a solid-gold pocket watch—you know, like a grandfather's watch—a beautiful little thing. And he had inscribed on it: 'To Big C from Little B.' That's what we used to call each other. I stood there and looked at it, and I simply couldn't speak for a while."

He went back to the couch, sat down, crossed his leg, didn't look at me. He had become very moved by the memory, and I remember feeling moved, too. There was a long pause.

He cleared his throat. "He's like that."

I waited a while, then continued softly. "Buddy once told me that he was the loneliest man in the universe. Do you often see him that way?"

"Yes, certainly, I take that for granted."

"Do you think it has anything to do with the fact that he's at the top of his profession?"

"Partly."

"Do *you* feel that way?"

"Often. You have to understand that we're in a business where insecurity is the prime common denominator. You're only as good as your last performance. It doesn't matter how high up you are; in fact, there's much more pressure at the top than there ever was on the way up. If you're Buddy Rich, people expect you to perform a hundred times better than any other drummer they've ever heard, and they expect it *every* performance. Nobody can tell you what makes Buddy the best drummer in the world—I'm sure *he* can't tell you, either. It's just something—it's a gift, it's not something that can be learned. Buddy can't teach it. But it's taken one hell of a lot of discipline to *perfect* that talent. He's been a professional for—what, over fifty years now. And he's been a perfectionist from the beginning. He expects every member of his band to give every bit of talent and energy they have, *every* time they play—just like he does. I mean, he doesn't ask them to do anything he doesn't do himself. He pushes them, he challenges them, he makes them strain, he makes them play better than they think they can. All this seems like a digression, I know, but I think it's part of the answer. Very few people strive for perfection the way he's always doing. He never lets up on himself. He expects everyone else to have the same fanatical devotion to quality that he has. And, of course, they don't. They just don't. Most musicians—most *people*—refuse to drive themselves that hard. As a result, I think the man is constantly frustrated by people, by their comparatively 'sloppy' approach to music, and, by extension, their oblivious attitude toward jazz musicians. He takes it personally. Consequently, and quite predictably, he doesn't have many friends."

"You're one of his few close friends, and yet, you two seem so dissimilar. At least, on the surface."

"Well, that's true. It probably started because I've always been a drummer, I've always been interested in drums. I still practice at home. So, I don't know, twenty years ago, I was listening to all the top drummers and Buddy was just miles ahead even then, he was just the best there was, beyond any question. So I suppose I was attracted to him, initially, because of that. But as time went on, we just had this good chemistry going. I mean, we could go a whole year without seeing each other and—you know, it seemed like yesterday. Like last month he came out here, and one day we spent about fifteen hours together, just talking. We had lunch, we had dinner, we sat around the house, laughing, clowning, and I hadn't seen him in months. I don't know what the hell it is, to answer your question. We're both very private individuals, we're both loners, neither of us have many close friends. We stay home. That's a fact. Maybe that's what we have in common, we're loners. We'd rather spend time with one or two close friends who are 'out front'—everything out front, no bullshit—than with a group of people, where we have to wear a mask, like they're wearing. Who needs it?"

The show was taped at 5:30 that afternoon, and it was particularly good, in my opinion. Johnny's other guests were Orson Bean, Dr. Joyce Brothers, and a young singer named Tom Sullivan, who had been blind from birth, and whose book, *If You Could See What I Hear*, had just been published and was going to be made into a feature film.

We got back to the hotel about 7:30, and Buddy's two sisters, Margie and Jo, who lived in Beverly Hills, and who had been at the studio for the show, came up to have dinner with us in the room. Margie was the eldest at sixty-four, very lean, tanned, with short but full white hair. Jo was sixty, a bit stout, but attractively so, also tanned, and wore her white hair in a pixie cut. We had drinks and talked, and Buddy clowned around with them. I remember he called Margie "Mag," and Jo "Fatso."

"Actually," Buddy told me, "I have a new nickname for these two old broads."

"Since last year," Mag said. "Now we're the 'Snoop Sisters.'"

"Because we like to be in on everything," Jo said.

Buddy laughed. "They not only have to be in on everything—"

"But I can't stand to be in the kitchen when everybody's talking," Mag interrupted.

"We had to go into the kitchen," Buddy explained. "If we're talking and she's cooking, we all had to troop out into the kitchen."

"Well, it was always like that," Jo said. "I mean, when we all lived together, before everyone was married and got out of the house. At first, when you got married, you moved in. We all had the bedrooms upstairs, and nobody was allowed to talk downstairs if it couldn't be heard upstairs. Everybody had to hear what was going on all over. And no matter where you were, you yelled."

"Wait'll *I* come in!" Mag said. "Wait'll *I* come in!"

"Right," Jo continued. "Don't talk till *I* get there!"

"Actually," Mag said, "we were never all home at once for any length of time, because we all traveled. But when we *were* at home, we all lived together, no matter whether we were married or not. In other words, the fact that we were married had nothing to do with separate lives. My husband and I, at the time we were married, we came and stayed with Dad and Mother. Jo, when she was married, stayed for a little while. On the occasions when we came home from being on the road, we all lived in one house and we had a ball."

"Sometimes we stayed with relatives," Jo added. "When we were very young."

Mag nodded. "I went to school in Albany, in Troy, in Schenectady, and in New York, because I stayed with one set of relatives and my sister stayed with my mother's relatives. And Mickey, for a little while, stayed with me up in Albany. But Buddy was always with my dad and mother, because he was always working. And he was really taking care of the family up until— well, he still takes care of my father. But when we worked, we chipped in whatever we could to help."

Jo rattled the ice in her glass, looked at it. "My father was always fond of saying, 'In this family, there's one pocket.'"

"Which was true," Mag agreed. "It was one for all and all for one. Whatever anybody earned, it all went into the pot."

Buddy cleared his throat. "I think I was twenty-two before I was allowed to keep any sizable amount."

"But the point was," Mag went on, "we could all *have* whatever we wanted. Daddy just wanted to be boss of the money."

"Like, in other words," Jo said, "I had to have a gown, a new gown, to work in. He went shopping with me. I might have seen something, we'll say, for a hundred dollars that I thought was very nice. He'd see one for a hundred and thirty dollars, he'd say, 'That's the one, because this is your bread and butter, you have to look the best you can look. That's the one you should have.' He didn't try to have us spend *less* money. We should all have the best of what we needed to have, particularly for work."

"Dad was the boss of the house," Mag said. "My mother was like one of us, rather than our mother." She glanced at Buddy. "You remember that?"

"Uh-huh."

"I mean, she was a marvelous mother, of course, but she didn't shop and cook and take care of us in the way that most normal kids are raised. She was used to being on the road with my father and she knew very little about housekeeping."

Jo had to laugh at that. "Most normal kids had nothing to do with us. We were the most—"

"*That's* true," Buddy said, smiling. "Most normal *people* had nothing in common with us."

Mag shrugged and laughed. "I think we all turned out fairly normal, even for our peculiarities."

"I resent that!" Jo snapped.

We all laughed. Buddy got out the room service menu and read the selections to us. We told him what we wanted and he went to the telephone.

"Mag," I said, "when you were working alone, what'd you do?"

"I was a dancer."

"What kind of dancer?"

"I worked in the chorus of shows the first five or six years I was in the business, then I met my husband and we did a dancing act together. I was married in nineteen thirty-three."

"I was a singer and comedienne," Jo said. She laughed, pointed to Buddy. "He never saw me work. He hasn't the slightest idea what I did."

Buddy was still waiting for room service to answer. "I *still* don't know what the hell you did."

"My sister was a singer and a comedienne," Mag told me. "But, actually, the comedienne comes first. She was very, very funny."

"I started out being a singer when I was thirteen," Jo said. "That was my first act, when I was thirteen. For the first couple of years I just sang, but my feeling was always for comedy, and I started to do comedy then, and the singing was secondary." She looked at Buddy, who was finally giving the order. "And I must tell you a very funny story which I know he won't remember. I'd been working for quite a few years, and not working any particularly good spots, or doing especially well, or as well as I'd hoped to do after working a few years. And there were no more theaters to play. Well, I *hated* nightclubs, and I thought, 'Well, maybe I'll just go back to singing.' But where're you going to go as a singer? Because, at this point, everything was vocalists with *bands*. And brother happened to come into town. This was about nineteen forty, and he was with Bunny Berigan. Came home, and he said he had a rehearsal the next day, and he wasn't looking forward to it, especially. Because Berigan was looking for a vocalist and they had to audition vocalists and do a lot of rehearsing, and then they were going on the road. I hear 'vocalist' and I don't say a word to him, but I call Berigan's manager and I say, 'I understand you're looking for a vocalist and I'd like to come up to sing for you.' Fine. He told me what time to be there. Now, I know their rehearsal is at one o'clock. Whenever brother was in town and *I* was in town, I would always go to his rehearsals. So it was perfectly natural and normal—from his point of view—to see me there. So I made the date and I get up there, and nobody's there yet, other than Berigan and the manager. And I had a little conversation with Gray, the manager, and I told him what I had done, that I'd been in the business but I'd never worked in a band. He said, 'Did you bring any music with you?' I said, 'Well, I know most of your charts.' So he mentioned a couple of tunes, and I said, 'Yes, I know them.'"

Buddy came back, sat down. "What lies you telling about me now?"

"When I auditioned for Berigan."

"Oh, *no*!"

"You don't *want* to remember *that* one."

"I remember it very clearly."

Jo sipped her drink, continued. "So I talked with Gray, he mentioned some tunes and I said I knew them. Well, with this, in comes my brother with two other musicians. He comes in, sees me, says, 'Oh, hi, Jo.' Tunes his drums, all the musicians come straggling in, tuning up, and Berigan says, 'All right, pull number one and take it from letter C,' which was the vocal. Brother sits down at the drums and I just can't look at him. So I have my back to him, and they play two bars before, to go into the vocal, and I start to sing—and I hear the sticks fall."

Buddy and Mag sat back and laughed.

"Right on the floor," Jo said, laughing too. "Well, Berigan says something to him, like, 'You're not awake yet, take it again.' And I sang three songs. Then they went on with the rehearsal and I talked to Gray. He said he had one other girl to sing that afternoon and he would call me to let me know. I didn't dare look at my brother, just a little wave, and out I went, back home. Well, within a few hours, I got a phone call to come in for rehearsal the next day, and I got the job. Six or seven that evening, in he comes. And I'm *flying*—'I got the *job*! I'm going to be on the *road* with you!' 'No, you're not.' 'What do you *mean*!—I just got a *call*, I got the *job*!' He says, 'I told Berigan that if you go on the road with the band, I won't.' '*Why*? What're you *doing* to me?' He gives me this look and he says, 'You think *I* want *my* sister traveling on a *bus* with eighteen *musicians*?'"

We all laughed hard, including Jo.

"I said, 'What do you *mean*, what've you got against *musicians*—*you're* a musician!' He says, 'That's what I *mean*!'"

I remember that really broke Buddy up, and we all laughed softly, watching him. The curtains were open and the wall and sliding door to the terrace were both floor-to-ceiling glass, and I could see mountains in the distance because it was still twilight.

Mag glanced at Buddy. "Remember the first time you joined Dorsey?"

"Yeah, in Chicago."

"You remember meeting Carl and me on the street, when you didn't stay at the rehearsal?" She turned to me: "Carl was my husband, Carl Ritchie."

Buddy nodded. "I told Dorsey I wouldn't be in the band , because it stunk."

"That's right." Mag turned to me again. "This was in nineteen forty-one, just before the war. Dorsey called him and said he was going to change the style of the band, and asked him to come to Chicago. And Carl and I were working around Chicago. And brother went to the first rehearsal. And Carl and I were walking down toward the hotel to see him play, and we met him on the street, and he was coming *back*. I said, 'The rehearsal's *over*?' He says, 'I'm not staying with that band.' He wasn't using bad language in those days, by the way."

"Not in front of *us*," Jo said.

Mag took a drink. "He didn't start using bad language until after the Marines. Anyway, he says he's not staying with the band. I said, 'Why?' He says, 'He's not playing my kind of music.' So, we went back to the hotel, and we sat around and talked. Dorsey calls, says, 'What happened?' Says, 'Listen, Sy Oliver is coming in to write, we're actually going to change the whole style of the band—come on back.' So he went back the next day and it began to happen. Sy Oliver wrote the first arrangement, *Losers Weepers*, and it began to happen."

"That's how the band changed," Buddy said quietly, leaning back. "That's how the band became great, they knew when to change. But it didn't happen overnight. God, I remember that first day in Chicago so vividly. Tommy's manager, Bobby Burns, he meets me, he says, 'You're going to love the band, we're making all the right changes, we're getting new blood, new life.' He says, 'Meet me downstairs in the Empire Room, we'll have dinner. This is in the Palmer House. Okay, fine. Went downstairs. Place was packed. People were dancing, everything. Band was—*terrible*. I mean, it was a nondescript band, you know, it didn't have any direction. It was a ballad band for Tommy's playing; it was a dance band, because it played at those fox-trot tempos. It had no individual sound. I heard about three or four tunes, I got up and I left. Bobby says, 'Where you going, what's the matter?' I said, 'I can't play with a band like that; you kidding?' He says, 'Well, look, we're rehearsing tonight, like you to play so you can get the feel of the band.' Okay, so I stayed. Stayed for about two or three tunes at the rehearsal, and I said, 'I'll see you.' I walked out. By accident, I ran into Mag and Carl in the street. I was going to catch a plane and go back to New York. And they couldn't understand it. They couldn't *believe* it. They thought I was out of my *skull*. 'Twenty-two years old, and you're telling *Tommy Dorsey* what kind of music to play?'" He paused, looked out the window. "That's right. I told him what to play and how to play it."

"All right, those were good times," Mag said. "Did you tell him about how broke we were at various times?"

Buddy smiled. "Oh, he knows."

"Which is just a part of everybody bunching together," she said.

"It was never very difficult," Buddy said, his eyes still on the window. "No matter how poor, in every sense of the word 'poor,' because I can remember..." He turned to Jo. "Tell him the story about the candles and Leo."

Jo laughed softly. "I had just met the man whom I later married, Leo Corday. He was a producer in the Catskill Mountains at that time, and I had just met him. Marg met her husband and I had met mine. We'd never been to the mountains before, and we were going to rehearse the show, because we were going away in two weeks."

"This was during one of our broke times," Mag said.

Jo frowned, trying to remember details. "I said to Leo, 'We have some rehearsing to do, why don't you come over to the house and we'll go through some things at home.' Not knowing that the lights were out."

"They'd shut off our electricity," Buddy said, enjoying it.

"The bill wasn't paid and there weren't any lights," Jo went on. "So, the doorbell rings, and there we are in the dark, with the candlelight showing through the windows. They open the door and it's Leo, and my father says—" She coughed, then deepened her voice, imitating him: "My father says, 'You'll have to excuse there not being any lights,' he says. 'I just went downstairs to the Super. There's something wrong with this line in the building, so there aren't any lights working, and I certainly hope they get them fixed before the night is over.' So, we passed that by, and Leo and I, we went to the kitchen, which is the smallest area, where you've got three or four candles, and you can see enough to read a script, you see. Brother and Mickey slept on a studio couch in the living room; my dad and mother had their bedroom; and there was another bedroom for Marge and I, whenever Marge came into town. So, Leo and I go into the kitchen and read the script." She gestured with her hands: "Now, there's the door coming into the room, and then a little, tiny foyer, and here's the kitchen, and here's the living room where the boys are asleep. And we're talking, and we hear this—" She stamped her feet on the floor, methodically. "Look up, and here's this flickering candle coming. Buddy's walking through the kitchen to the bathroom, looking straight ahead, holding the candle. Bathroom door closes. Candlelight flickers under the door. Toilet flushes. Door opens. Back he comes, thump, thump, thump, through the kitchen, his little face glowing in the candlelight, looking straight ahead. Well, it must've happened twenty times that night. He wasn't ready to go to *sleep*, you see, and he wasn't allowed to stay up, because we were very busy rehearsing here, you know, so he had to sit in the dark, way before his *bedtime*. What was he going to *do*? All he *could* do was go back and forth to the bathroom, *hoping* that someone would engage him in a conversation, so that he didn't have to go to *bed*."

"Tell him about Oscar," Buddy said. "Tell him about 'The Skeleton.'"

Jo rolled her eyes to the ceiling. "That was on West One Hundred Eighth Street. We were living in a furnished apartment. We had just been put out of our house, and my father borrowed some money from a friend, and we rented this furnished apartment. It was a walk-up, but it was lovely. That's where we used to stretch out on the floor and listen to the radio. I remember I was sixteen then—so that would've made Buddy thirteen. Let's see, that would make it nineteen thirty. Anyhow, there was this walk-up, and a *steep* flight of stairs, and a little square landing, and the door was right here. Now, I was expecting this boy to come up to call on me, who had never met my family. His name was Oscar and he was very skinny and he wanted to marry me. He was thirteen and he looked exactly like James Cagney. *Exactly*. Well, Buddy and my father were always playing tricks on everybody that I had over. So I said, 'Now, listen, this boy is coming, he's *very* shy, he's *very* quiet. I don't want *any*body to say *any*thing to scare him. He's really *very* nice, so no tricks.' The doorbell rings and I want to get to the door before either of them, even my father. No way. No chance. My father opens the door. Brother was here, and my father was here, and I'm over here. And I say, 'Oscar, I'd like you to meet my dad.' 'How do you do, Mr. Rich,' he shakes hands. 'And my brother Buddy.' And my brother shakes hands, and he's got a *buzzer* in his palm, you know, the kind that you wind up? The guy was so shocked, he fell over *backwards* down the steep flight of stairs! God, I can see him now, tumbling head-over-heels down those stairs! Never heard from him again."

Jo laughed softly, leaned forward to me. "I have to tell you the story about the first band Buddy had, when he was fourteen years old."

"We were at the hotel," Mag said. She looked at Buddy. "You remember that?"

"Hotel America," he said. "West Forty-seventh Street."

"It was during the time there were breadlines," Jo said quietly. "There was just no money around. This was nineteen thirty-one. Marge and I were working an act, sending home every cent we could spare. The last week's work was canceled. It was during the summer and theaters were closing; they didn't have air conditioning at that time. We come home, we go to the hotel with our suitcases. We get into the elevator, we hear this music that's so loud that the walls are shaking. I said, 'God, somebody's got their radio on *awful* loud.' We're coming up to our floor in the elevator and the music gets louder as we go *up*. We get off at our floor and the music is so loud we can't believe it. It's coming from *our* room. Open the door, here's *thirteen men*, on the chairs, on the tables, on the floor—Buddy with the drums—and they're *rehearsing*!"

Buddy cracked up at that, clapping his hands.

"My father had passed this breadline," Jo went on, "and got into a conversation with a young man who was on the breadline, who told him a very sad story about how he'd come into town with a band, and the leader skipped with the money and left them all stranded. They were all from Pittsburgh and they didn't have a nickel. Anyhow, while talking with him, my father got this fantastic idea: Here was a set band, brother's not doing anything, why doesn't he take this band and put brother up in front of it? He wasn't 'Buddy' at that time, he was 'Pal,' my father used to call him 'Pal.' Why not put Pal up in front of it—and maybe he could get some *work*! All they needed was just a few days of rehearsal and he could get them *booked*. They weren't booking brother as a single at that time. He was at that very awkward age, fourteen, when he wasn't a little kid any more, but he wasn't a man yet. And, sure enough, they *did* get work! Buddy's first band. But the guys said they only wanted to work long enough to get enough money together to make their fare to go back home."

"We had this two-room suite at the hotel," Mag said. "And a couple of the boys had some friends they stayed with in Jersey, and I think there were about seven or eight of them stayed in the hotel, slept on the floor in the living room. And we had a little two-burner gas range, and my daddy used to make egg sandwiches."

"Scrambled eggs," Jo said. "The manager of the hotel, our daddy had gotten very friendly with him, so he pretended he didn't smell all this cooking going on, you know?"

"Daddy used to stand and make egg sandwiches," Mag said. "That's where our *money* went that we were sending home!"

"Eggs to feed the boys," Jo said. "Bags of sweet rolls, cartons of milk."

"It was weird," Buddy told me. "For a family like this, nothing was ever catastrophic. Being poor was part of the game, and being rich was part of the game, then being poor again." He paused, glanced at his sisters. "On the plane yesterday, John was asking questions about Lana Turner. I think I mentioned that she used to come into New York to play the Paramount." He looked at me, smiled. "One time, she called me and said she was coming in, and I said, 'Will you stay at the house in Brooklyn?' She says, 'Sure.' So I told my family, I said, 'Listen, try to straighten up around the house and behave yourselves.'"

Jo laughed. "I had to redecorate the bedroom."

"We used to have a number around the house," Buddy said. "Where, if you looked like you were pretty straight, we would take you around and show you the house, then drop you in the shower and turn the water on—fully clothed."

"No matter *what* you had on," Jo added.

Buddy nodded. "And no matter *who* it was. So I said, 'That game is over, Lana Turner is coming out.' Of course, they all knew about the romance and everything. So, I don't know how it got out, man, but all *Brooklyn* knew that Lana Turner was staying at Buddy Rich's house. Okay, I met her at the airport, drove her in." He looked at Jo. "How long was she in the house before she had her bath?"

"Not very long."

"She wasn't in the house half an hour before we stuck her in the shower."

"I want you to know," Mag told me, "that *I* didn't *do* these things."

"No," Jo agreed. "Marg didn't participate in things like this."

"Zap, right in the shower," Buddy said. "Gorgeous lady."

"I have to tell you about Mickey's reaction to this," Jo said. "Brother and I went to the airport to get her. Now, here's a big movie star coming to the house. Gorgeous, breathtaking. So we all get *dressed*, you know, we're not going to sit around like *schleps*. We get all dressed and we hear them drive up and we all go over to the door. Mickey is here, I'm here alongside of him, and Marge is on the other side of him. Mickey's got his arms around our shoulders. The door opens, and here's this lady, *no* makeup, with a scarf tied around her head, sloppy gray-flannel slacks and a gray-flannel sweatshirt—not a sweater, but a sweat-shirt, like a jogging outfit—and so utterly beautiful that she was almost *unbelievable*. And here *we* are, with the eyes made up, faces made up, all dressed to kill. Brother introduces her, and Mickey looks at her, turns around and looks at us, and his expression says it all, I'll never forget it, like, 'You know, I got two of the ugliest sisters in the world.'"

Buddy laughed, lit a cigarette, narrowed his eyes. "The thing was that when word got around—like, in two minutes, you know—that Lana Turner was staying at the house, the house became like a *museum*. Packs of kids would walk by, hoping they could catch a glimpse of her. And she was so cool, so completely unpretentious, that when she'd go outside for a stroll or something, she'd wear old clothes, she'd stand around, sign autographs, talk with the kids, you know, absolutely nothing bothered her."

It went on like that through dinner; I enjoyed it immensely, and I think they did, too. Mag and Jo went home about eleven o'clock, and Buddy and I watched the news, and then *The Tonight Show* at 11:30.

He had suspected that he wasn't quite as sharp as usual for the show and, as he observed his conversation with Johnny, he seemed convinced of it and became progressively more depressed as the show went along. For one thing, he'd worn a blue blazer, shirt and tie, which was unusual for him, and he'd felt too formal. For another, he thought the conversation lingered too long on his broken finger. There were a lot of things he'd planned to say, but he didn't, primarily because his reactions simply weren't as fast as they normally were. The only thing he seemed fairly satisfied with was his drum solo. He didn't say so, but his eyes did.

After the show, he opened the glass door to the terrace, went out there, closed the door. In the soft glow of the lamp near the door, I could see him leaning against the railing. I waited a while, then switched off the television, lit a cigarette, and joined him. It was warm after the air conditioning, and dark, and I remember hearing distant traffic noises. He was still leaning against the railing, his arms rigid, looking down at the sparkling sprawl of streets and house lights in the valley, which seemed to pulsate in the heat.

"You want a cigarette?" I asked softly.

He shook his head slowly, negatively.

"You just weren't that bad, Buddy. Honest to God."

"I'm going to write a letter of apology to Johnny."

"Apology for what?"

"For ruining his whole show."

He said it so softly that I could hardly hear. We stood there in silence for several minutes. He was gripping the railing so tightly that I could see the veins in his hands. I wanted to help him, but it was difficult to find the words. I wanted to tell him what Carson had said about him in our talk that afternoon, but I knew it wouldn't do any good.

"You understand this crazy life?" he asked quietly.

I hesitated. "No."

"It's crazy."

"You expect too much from yourself, Buddy."

"No, I don't."

"And you expect too much from others."

He looked at me for the first time, sideways, then glanced away. "You understand me any better than you did when we met?"

"I think so."

"That's good. Marie doesn't, Cathy doesn't, my family thinks they do, but they don't. They don't even have the first idea. Sometimes I think *nobody* ever really gets to understand *anybody* else. Which is a horrible thought. At least, to me it is. We're locked up inside our own bodies for life. Solitary confinement for life. We scream inside ourselves, but nobody seems to hear. We're born alone, we try to communicate with other people all our lives, and fail mostly, and then we die alone. It's crazy."

"Maybe the only crazy thing is to *expect* more."

"Well, I do," he said, almost in a whisper. "That's the wild thing. I expect a hell of a lot more. And I'm going to keep screaming at myself, and at others, until I get more. Because, when I stop screaming, I'm dead."

11

THAT AUTUMN OF 1974, Buddy's European concert tour started in the middle of October and included cities in Italy, England, Scotland, and Ireland. I was with him for most of the dates around England—Croydon, Portsmith, London, Oxford, and one in Edinburgh, but the night he played the Royal Albert Hall in London stands out more clearly in my mind than any of the others. It was Wednesday, October 23, and the London newspapers had bold headlines about a bomb explosion at the exclusive 210-year-old Brooks Club in the West End, which was just opposite a club where Conservative leader Edward Heath was dining. *The Daily Mail* also had a juicy front-page story, with photographs, revealing the latest shocks in the sordid saga of Miss Rachel Fitler, a multi-millionaire American spinster who agreed to marry Mike Wilson, a twenty-nine-year-old Welsh bartender. Shock one occurred the previous night when Miss Fitler, an aunt of Happy Rockefeller, told the truth about her age: she was not sixty-one, as she had claimed all along, but seventy-seven! Shock two came when she refused, after a meeting with her physician and attorney, to say if the wedding was still on! Well, as you can imagine, the suspense was almost too much to bear.

Meanwhile, *Melody Maker*, the influential music newspaper, which claimed a readership of 1.6 million per week, had just hit the stands with a shockingly mean three-column photograph of

Buddy Rich, looking like he was about to eat you alive. It was a long article and I had to laugh out loud when I read the beginning:

Big Bad Buddy Rich is back in town—
and claiming that he was misunderstood.
Those Osmonds remarks were only a joke,
he tells CHRIS WELCH

"THEY say that I get mad all the time, but if they took the time to find out about people, and not rely on what Charley tells them, there would be a much greater relationship." Buddy Rich, sipping tea in the lounge of the London Hilton, was in a reflective mood, uncharacteristic, if you believe what Charley tells you.

The hellraiser and man with the damaging wit was calm, friendly and not in the least egotistical. The same Buddy Rich, in fact, who first met the MM back at the Hilton in 1967—and who has been regularly touring Britain since with his successful big band. Now Buddy is making his first ever appearance here with a small group and was wondering what the sound and reaction would be like.

Through a pair of rather hip, tinted spectacles, he smiled as he recalled his hectic years on the road, and his propensity to upset the sensitive. "Last time I was here, I was told to go home," he said, referring to an MM front-page story which took him to task over his remarks about the Osmonds on Michael Parkinson's TV show.

"I thought people over here had a sense of humor. I was only joking when I called the little guy a midget. But if you want me to make a serious statement about the Osmonds, I'll sit down and talk about them." I thought it would be more interesting to hear about Buddy Rich...

From that point on, the "Big Bad Buddy" angle was dropped, but it was amusing to see how Chris Welch, one of the most respected jazz writers in Britain, had used it as a news peg to draw attention. I'd met Chris the previous Sunday, October 20, at Fairfield Hall in Croydon, and talked with him at some length during a backstage party after the concert. The large, modern hall, with a seating capacity of 2,000, had been completely sold out, as it always was when Buddy played, and there had been an orderly line of more than 100 autograph seekers (I counted) after the show, starting at his dressing room door and extending all the way out the stage door.

"It may be difficult to understand," Chris told me, "but for the past five years or so, Buddy's been more popular here than in America. He was a legendary figure long before he started appearing here. We take it for granted that he's a great musician, but he adds an extra dimension—he has a reputation for show-manship. In a curious way, I think the 'Big Bad Buddy' image actually enhances his reputation. He'll probably sell out every theater he plays on this tour, with the possible exception of Albert Hall."

Chris was right about the enormous Albert Hall, but I think the weather helped to cut the crowd somewhat. I had been staying with my mother-in-law, Phyllis Hill, in West Kensington, and when we took a taxi to the concert on Wednesday evening, it was cold, windy, and starting to rain. All along Kensington High Street people were bundled up, leaning against the wind and rain, and the trees in Kensington Gardens, across from the Hall, were losing masses of leaves. Phyllis was seventy-four that year, but didn't look anywhere near it, and she was as lively as ever that evening, 118 pounds of energy, with pure white hair in a super new do. She had been a jazz fan since the 1920s, had seen Buddy perform several times at Ronnie Scott's club in London, and had insisted on going to Buddy's Place when she was in New York in September. She was something else.

I picked up our tickets at the box office and we met my wife's sister, Wendy Lawson, with her husband, Ashley, and their two children, Charlotte and Jolyon. Phyllis, Wendy, and Ashley went upstairs to our box; I took Charlotte and Jolyon outside, around to the stage door, and into Buddy's large and handsomely furnished dressing room, which was filled with people.

Buddy was there, signing autographs, in very good spirits, looking trim in a new white cashmere turtleneck, and wearing the solid-gold "dog tag" that Cathy had given him September 30, on his fifty-seventh birthday. It was inscribed:

HAPPY BIRTHDAY
DADDY   9/30/74
I LOVE YOU
CATHY

For about seven years before that, he had worn an Egyptian ankh as a pendant, a tau cross with a loop at the top, which ancient Egyptians used as a symbol of generation or enduring life, and when he lost it, he felt profoundly depressed, because it had been a gift from Marie and had tremendous sentimental value. Cathy understood, withdrew almost all her savings to buy the new pendant, and, from that night on, I never saw him without Cathy's beautiful gift around his neck.

Buddy made a big fuss over Charlotte and Jolyon and had them sit down and join the conversation. They were really great kids and they couldn't have been happier. Charlotte was fifteen then, "going on twenty-one," tall, graceful, with long tawny blonde hair. She was a talented ballet dancer and actress, resembled a young Liv Ullmann, and had actually been invited to casting sessions for the role of Queen Christina as a child in the Warner

Bros. film *The Abdication*, starring Liv Ullmann and Peter Finch. Although she performed well before the director, Anthony Harvey, the part eventually went to a younger actress. Jolyon's main claim to fame at age thirteen was that he owned his own car, a rare 1932 Singer, one of only three custom jobs built in that year. Bought it himself, fixed it up, planned to sell it for a fortune.

Leo Ruocco was there, of course, standing by the door, admitting people for autographs, two-by-two, and Buddy was flanked by Eddie Kennedy of Kennedy-Masters Ltd., the promoter of the tour, with his fiancee, Mary Teng, an old friend from New York who was living in London, and Sid Cross of LBC Radio, who was preparing his equipment for an interview, as Buddy signed the last of the autograph books and programs.

Sid sat next to Buddy, turned on his tape recorder and held up the microphone. "Buddy, let's get a level on this. The Albert Hall with Buddy Rich. Hello, Buddy Rich; hello, hello, hello, Buddy Rich. And now Buddy Rich says hello."

"Hello, Sidney Cross; hello, Sidney Cross; hello, Sidney Cross. Mayday, Mayday, Mayday."

There was a loud knock on the door and Leo greeted Les Tompkins of *Crescendo* magazine, who was also scheduled for an interview.

"Come on in," Buddy said. "Hello, Les Tompkins; hello, Les Tompkins; hello, Les Tompkins. We're going on the air; come in and sit down."

"We won't mention the day," Sid told Buddy, "we'll just say we're celebrating your birthday, which is the truth."

"Right."

Sid held up his hand for quiet. "Hello, Buddy, greetings from all of LBC and London on your visit here at Albert Hall. On your birthday, not so long ago, we all celebrated the fact that you are now fifty-six years old."

Buddy nodded. "Fifty-seven, to be exact."

"No kidding?"

"Honest to God."

"Fifty-seven. At fifty-seven, a lot of musicians—pianists, what have you—can take it easy and continue playing, but not often do you hear of fifty-seven-year-old drummers who continue working as hard as you appear to do. And I know you do."

"Well, actually, I don't work that hard, Sid, and I never contemplate the age factor in playing music. I just think that as long as you can play, you should play. And being fifty-seven is no different. I think I'm playing better today at fifty-seven than I played at twenty-seven, so there's something to say about old age."

"I'm sure that's true. Now, can we just run back for a few years and see if I can get something original that has never been written or spoken about before. In nineteen thirty-eight, you were with the Bunny Berigan band, which is considered a legend in jazz. Is there anything in that particular era that stays with you?"

Buddy played it poker-faced. "Oh, sure. In nineteen thirty-eight, I was *not* with Bunny Berigan. That stays with me. I was with Joe Marsala in nineteen thirty-eight. And in nineteen thirty-nine, I joined Bunny Berigan and I stayed with him six months, and then I went with Artie Shaw and I stayed with him for about a year. Then I went with Dorsey."

"When you were with Dorsey, you were contemporary with Frank Sinatra, right? What were your feelings about that Slim Jim then?"

"I thought then that he was the greatest singer I'd ever heard, and I was fortunate enough to be present at his concert at Madison Square Garden several weeks ago, and my opinion hasn't changed one bit. He's still the greatest singer in the world."

"So, they were pretty happy days with the Tommy Dorsey band."

"Oh, they were happy on occasion, but mostly unhappy. Touring with that band for as many years as I did, I can't look back on too many joyous occasions. I look back at it as a very hard time in my life."

"What would you consider to be the peak, the happiest time, as far as music is concerned?"

"I consider the happiest part of my life what I'm doing right now. I look forward to days like this, nights like this, and I look forward to the future. I think this is my ninth time in London, and I think that everything that we do is part of the next step, going forward."

"Well, that's interesting; it prompts a thought from me. You have how many pieces here—eight?"

"Six and myself, seven altogether."

"Seven pieces, but we've heard you in London working with fifteen, sixteen pieces over the years. Now, if you had carte blanche, if someone came along and said, 'I'm going to sponsor Buddy Rich in whatever idea he comes up with, with regard to music,' what would you do?"

"Exactly what I'm doing. Playing the things that I like to play. The reason I don't ever look forward to having someone sponsor me is that you always have to bend to somebody else's wishes, whether they be musical or financial."

"No, I didn't mean that. I merely meant that if you had a total free course as to the way you could chart your directions."

"Well, Sid, that would never involve another man, then. That would strictly involve me and my taste and my choice of musicians, and I've been doing that all my life, and I've been fairly successful with it, and I hope to continue along that line. I choose the musicians, I choose the music that we play, and I choose how to play it. That way, I have nobody to fall out on and say, 'You were wrong.' If I'm wrong, I take all the heat; if I'm right, I take all the credit. And I prefer it that way."

"You're very serious tonight, Buddy. We've had interviews when you were really sidesplitting."

He smiled, nodded. "I'm not terribly sidesplitting tonight. I'm getting ready to go on and I kind of relax this way. I don't feel very humorous at this point. When I get on the stage and I feel that the audience is receptive and responsive to what I have to say, then I change, of course."

"I suppose you're going to be coming back with the big band again."

"No, actually, I'm coming back in April with a quartet. You see, this tour was originally set to be with Lionel Hampton, Teddy Wilson, George Duvivier, and myself. And, as you might know, Lionel Hampton was taken very seriously ill last month, had a very serious operation, and he's resting right now. We'll be coming back with that quartet."

"So this touring life doesn't bother you, really, you get fun out of it."

"The only thing that bothers me is when I have to stay in one place too long. I like to travel, I like to meet new people, I like to get an idea what's going on in the world. I'm a road man."

"What's the relaxation you really go for, look forward to, when you're traveling around so?"

Buddy thought about it. "Sleep."

Sid turned from the microphone, laughed out loud. "Is that why nobody can get through to you before four o'clock in the afternoon?"

"Something like that. Actually, when I'm home, I'm very heavily into karate. And other times I'm with my daughter and my wife, we go out and almost behave like human beings."

"I've always known you to be very human, very dedicated, very humorous, and I hope you'll continue to enjoy life. Come and see us here in London as often as you can, because you know that you've got a tremendous fan pool here."

"Yes, I appreciate that, too. I love it over here and that's not show biz talk. I really do love it over here, and probably one day, when I'm fed up with New York City and all of the things that happen there, if I could get my wife to get out of her shops long enough, why, I may just hop on a plane and come back here and live."

"And I'll look out for a castle for you."

We could hear music as the interview ended. The way the program was set up throughout the tour, pianist Teddy Wilson went on first with his own trio, which included British musicians Peter Chapman on bass and Derek Hogg on drums. I glanced at my watch: 7:30. As Sid Cross was gathering up his equipment, Les Tompkins took his place and started the interview for *Crescendo*.

I wished Buddy luck, left with Charlotte and Jolyon, went around to the lobby and upstairs to our box, number seventeen in the Grand Tier, which could accommodate about twelve people and provided an excellent view of the stage. Teddy Wilson's gentle, melodic style was delightful and the acoustics were superb.

Seeing the interior of Royal Albert Hall for the first time was, I admit, rather mind-blowing. Although the seating capacity was only 3,500, it seemed positively enormous. Constructed nearly a century ago, its Victorian architecture and furnishings appeared to have been derived mainly from Baroque and Gothic styles, characterized by heavy carved ornament, elaborate moldings, and dark varnished woodwork. The "area" floor ("orchestra" section to Americans) was surrounded by four elliptical tiers—termed stalls, boxes, balcony, and gallery—reaching to a lofty domed ceiling, where massive chandeliers provided a high percentage of the house lighting. At the rear of the stage was an organ with gigantic gold-colored pipes extending to the ceiling. Although I couldn't see many empty seats when the houselights came on at the end of Teddy Wilson's portion of the concert, I learned later than the official paid attendance was around 2,500.

After the intermission, it was time for Buddy's band and, if he had any doubts about the receptiveness of the crowd, they were obliterated at the moment he walked out on stage. Conceding the famed British propensity for understatement, even the most conservative critic would have called that initial standing ovation "extraordinary" for staid old Albert Hall, and it clearly helped set the mood for the rest of the evening.

Looking back, I don't remember Buddy becoming more responsive to another audience on that tour, with the exception of his concert in Edinburgh on October 26, when he threw his tough-guy image to the Scottish winds and surprised a sold-out Usher Hall by walking on stage replete in a striking red Stuart kilt. Before he could hide behind his tom-toms, the Scots gave him a shouting, whistling, standing tribute; approximately twenty people actually rushed to the stage to shake his hand and women—young and old—kissed him. When things settled down, he told the audience: "To be honest about it, I was a little scared to perform in drag, but, really, this is cool as hell, especially when I sit down."

Albert Hall wasn't like that, but the vibrations were extremely warm and the band was noticeably "up" from the start. The lineup for that tour included all the regulars from the club— Bunch, Nistico, Romano, Wilkins, Allende—but Bob Cranshaw had again replaced Anthony Jackson on bass. Like most European crowds, the one that night remained virtually silent through each number, saving their appreciation until each chart was completely finished, and that was refreshing. They were really *listening*:

Listening to the subtleties and shadings, listening to the solos and transitions, listening to Buddy's craftsmanship with the brushes as well as the sticks; listening, eventually, to his solo, in which nothing was held back for that audience, absolutely nothing.

After the curtain calls, after the encores, after the final, loud, long, emotional ovation, when it was all over, there was such a mob scene outside at the stage door that I couldn't even get close. I had to go back into the Hall, climb the stage, and push through to his dressing room. He had showered and changed by then and was rushing to make an eleven o'clock live interview at Capitol Radio.

Just as he was about to leave, Carl Palmer came in with his attractive girlfriend, Maureen. I had heard Buddy speak a great deal about Carl and it was the first time I had met him. He was twenty-four that year, an exceptionally good-looking kid, lean, wiry, strong, dark brown hair fairly long and curly, dressed unpretentiously in a navy-blue jacket over a black crew-neck sweater and dark trousers. Of all the young drummers Buddy had observed over the past five years, Carl was his personal choice as the most promising, and they had developed a rather close relationship, getting together whenever they could; for example, Buddy had spent that entire afternoon at Carl's place in Arkley. Carl's rock group, "Emerson, Lake and Palmer," was among the most popular in Britain at that time, and five of its records had sold in excess of one million copies each.

Buddy wanted Carl and Maureen to accompany us to Capitol Radio; then, after the interview, we would all go over to the One Hundred Club to catch "The World's Greatest Jazz Band" show. We hurried out, but when Leo opened the stage door, the crush was so great that Buddy had to duck inside. He sat at a table near the door and Leo took charge, letting people in two at a time. Most wanted autographs, some took pictures, and the procession became quite organized and orderly. Eddie Kennedy kept glancing at his watch, worried that we wouldn't make the radio show; finally, he told his chauffeur, John Turner, to drive the car up the alley to the stage door. When we heard the car's horn, we walked out quickly, Buddy still signing autographs; Eddie, Mary Teng, Leo, and I jumped in, followed by Buddy, and Carl and Maureen ran for their car.

John Turner was actually a freelance chauffeur hired frequently by Kennedy-Masters Ltd. to transport artists around the country during concert tours. A short, stocky, bald Australian with a terrific sense of humor, Turner was a former stock car racing driver, and he proved it that night. His gray Mercedes had every electronic gadget available back then, including a telephone, a stereo tape deck that was constantly in use, and a television set facing the back seat. Although the streets were still wet and we were making plenty of sharp turns, I remember feeling perfectly confident with John at the wheel. He had the rhythms and reflexes of a well-conditioned athlete.

We arrived at Capitol Radio, Euston Tower, about 10:55, and I was really surprised to see Carl's old Rolls-Royce pull up behind us, because John had taken every shortcut he knew. We hurried in, signed the guard's book, and went upstairs. Buddy was shown into the studio immediately and began a leisurely interview with Sara Ward, who was hosting the show. She wore earphones, spoke very softly, introduced Buddy by playing a Mel Tormé record, *All I Need is a Girl*, then held her own in a half-hour conversation, interspersed with selections from a variety of Buddy's albums.

It was all very relaxed and pleasant, but as Buddy was coming out of the studio, he was approached by Nick Slater, a young writer with *Drums and Percussion* magazine. He was clean-cut and very polite.

"Mr. Rich, are you about set for our interview?" Slater asked.

"What interview?"

"We were told that you'd agreed to talk with us right after Sara Ward."

"Well, I'm afraid you were misinformed," Buddy told him.

"We arranged it through Kennedy-Masters."

"No way."

"May I ask why?"

"Because I think your magazine is absolutely terrible, one of the worst in the industry."

Nick took it in stride. "Well, fair enough, why not talk about that? Why not tell us why?"

Buddy considered it. "If I did it, I'd say it all—you understand that? I wouldn't pull any punches."

"Fair enough."

"Let's do it, let's make it fast."

We followed Nick along a series of corridors and into an office. His wife was there with a tape recorder. One thing I'll have to say about Nick, he was cool. He couldn't have been more than twenty-one, but from the opening minutes, when they sat down and really went at it, he remained as calm and collected as you please, never interrupted, never seemed in the least defensive. I remember him leaning forward, listening, his brown hair thick but trim, wearing a short-sleeved dark gray sport shirt, muscular arms braced on his knees. Although he had two pages of written questions, he discarded them and played it strictly by ear, which seemed to impress Buddy, because the conversation was extremely technical. Nick was a drummer himself, an eloquent spokesman for the magazine, with questions that were technically complicated, sensitive, and probing. An interview that could have been a heated five-minute argument had developed into a forty-five minute discussion with a give-and-take that Buddy clearly enjoyed. Carl Palmer stuck his head in the door several times and

Buddy told him he'd be right out, but then he got deeply involved in the conversation each time. We finally left about 12:30. And, as it turned out, *Drums and Percussion* magazine had a cover story to beat anything they had published in years.

The One Hundred Club, 100 Oxford Street, was a private club in the basement of a building situated between Tutnam Court Road and Oxford Circus. When we parked and went downstairs, it was probably close to one o'clock, but the large room was crowded, smoke-filled, and you could hardly hear yourself speak over the blasting Dixieland sounds of "The World's Greatest Jazz Band," which was also represented by Kennedy-Masters Ltd. As you entered, there was a long bar to the right with people three-deep, the bandstand was in the center against the wall, and a Chinese food bar was doing a good business at the far end. Eddie, Mary, Leo, John, and I went to the bar; Buddy took Carl and Maureen off in a corner to talk.

Before ten minutes had passed, the bandleader announced Buddy's arrival, gave him a tremendous introduction, and asked him to sit in for a number. I could tell Buddy didn't want to, but with all the applause and shouting he had to oblige. They played *Sweet Georgia Brown*, and Buddy's solo brought the house down. Watching him work, with the sweat dripping, I remember wondering, as always, where the hell he found the energy to extend himself that long, but particularly after playing a complete concert only a few hours before.

Afterward, he was surrounded by people and I thought it would be a good opportunity to get acquainted with Carl Palmer. With the band playing, you really couldn't talk in the room, so we went upstairs and sat on the top step. It was a lot cooler there and the music was muffled enough so that we didn't have to raise our voices.

"Buddy's told me quite a bit about you," I told him, "and one of the things he mentioned was the first time you met in London, when you came to his hotel. How old were you then, about sixteen?"

He spoke softly with a very slight cockney accent. "Yes, I was about sixteen at the time and he was staying at the Dorchester. I'd never met him, but he's a man that I'd always admired. First started playing the drums, he was the cat that I'd always followed, and I was determined to meet him and chat to him and discuss drums and things. So I went into the hotel and I said, 'Could I speak to Mr. Rich, please?' So they said, 'Are you a friend of his?' I said, 'Yes, a big friend.' I figured this was the only way, to lie through my teeth, you know? So they tried to throw me out, because I had like long hair and I was scruffy and, you know, I hadn't got a lot of money."

"This was what year?"

"This would be—I was sixteen—this would be sixty-six. So it's quite a while ago. Anyway, they said, 'Okay, we'll call his room.' They called his room and he wasn't there. And I turned 'round, and the elevator doors opened, and there he was, the man I'd always wanted to see." He smiled like a little kid, remembering, and his eyes widened. "It was fabulous, it was just the way it should've been. If it was going to happen, that's the way it would've happened. And he walked out, and I shook his hand, and I had a record and he put his name on the record for me, the album sleeve—and from then the relationship grew and grew. The following day I went back to the hotel and I spent some time with him and it just escalated from there."

"Did he teach you significant things about drumming, right from the beginning?"

"Yes, from the first day I ever met him, he's given me some kind of advice that's been valid. He's always shown me things, talked about things—had deep conversations. In many things, you know, besides music, he's been a kind of *father*, in a way. I sort of look on him as somebody I can listen to, or even talk to, about any kinds of problems I have, as far as music, as far as developing as a musician. And he's been through it all, so he understands one hundred percent *exactly* how a young up-and-coming drummer—after *his* goal—would feel. And once you get to know the man, I find him to be one of the warmest characters you could ever meet. People always talk about the *arrogant* Buddy Rich, but that's—"

"It's kind of surface."

"It really is so *surface*. I'm not saying the man couldn't be arrogant if he wanted to—as we all know, he can—but he's the most lovable, the most—kindest cat you could ever want to meet."

"He has very few friends, because he's very selective about them."

"And so he should be, you know? I think that Buddy goes for pureness in people. He'll go for somebody who has like pure content, not somebody who wants to be his friend because of who he is. I must confess, when *I* first met him, obviously I was overwhelmed by his playing and I wanted to play like him and, you know, look like him and everything. I mean, you must realize that somebody like that was my idol, and still is. But after speaking to the person, getting to know him *really* well, one then understands that there's more than just drumming there, there's a sincere person, and I think that's reflected in his playing and that's one of the reasons he's so good. But not only in drumming is he sincere, but in everything that he does. He's a very pure person. And when you say that he's very selective about the friends that he chooses—yes, because he looks for everyone to be as sincere as he is."

Carl had to move out of the way for some people who were coming up the stairs.

I pushed over against the wall. "You probably heard how upset Cathy was about that article in the recent *Cue*."

"Oh, yes."

"He made a comment about your group that was taken completely out of context and he—"

"Yes, he told me, ridiculous."

"He almost didn't know how to approach it. He said, 'You know, I'm going to talk with Carl and explain exactly what I *did* say, exactly what was taken out of context.' I hope you understand what happened."

"Yes. I haven't read the particular interview that you're talking about."

"It isn't much, really. I read it and I was surprised that it was that little."

"I'm surprised that even a fuss was made about the interview that he did, because I hope he knows that I'd see through that sort of thing. If I'd read the interview, I'd realize straight away that it was a misquote, because I've had it happen to me many, many times, and I'm sure he's had it happen to him billions of times. So I was quite amazed, but I appreciated that. It was nice, but he didn't have to do it. As far as I'm concerned, he doesn't have to explain anything to me."

"He was telling me in the car tonight that he wished he'd had the time, when he was your age, to really study the fine technicalities of the craft. Do you work when you're home, study quite a bit?"

"Oh, yes. Well, I'm studying at the moment at the Royal Academy of Music here. I'm studying with James Blade, who's the professor of percussion there, and I've been studying with him quite a while now."

"How long?"

"Twelve months. I've had another teacher called Gilbert Webster, from the Guild Hall of Music. I study quite a lot. I've never done anything else in my life, you know? I feel, at this stage, I've reached a kind of peak in England, where I have sort of recognition within this small country. But I think I have to go on now and learn a lot more, and that's what I'm doing at the moment. I'm learning composition, and how to conduct, and how to do all these other things that I'm sure Buddy would like to do."

"He would have loved to."

"The thing is, he has a little more—*gift* for playing the instrument. There's no doubt that I could, at some time in my career, come *near* to what he's doing. There's no doubt about that in my own mind, and I think he probably knows that. How near, how close, I'll never know. For me, it will be hard work all the way along the line, so it's my perseverance that will make the point. With him, it's always been natural, so he's very fortunate."

"Your group now has four platinum records and one gold?"

"No, five platinum records."

"Gold represents a million sales, then platinum—"

"Gold comes first, then after you get over a million and a half to two million, they become platinum. And we're the kind of group that has what they call a very large back-catalogue. What this means is, we sell a lot of records when it first comes out, but it doesn't die away, it keeps on a constant—rotor." He glanced at me, smiled with the enthusiasm of a little boy. "And that's obviously good for business, it's good for record companies, and it's good for us."

"And you're how old right now?"

"I'm twenty-four."

"Do you feel that getting this, this early, could be detrimental?"

"Getting albums?"

"Getting this far, this early. This much money, this much recognition."

He paused, looking down the stairs, blinking, listening to the muted Dixieland. "The recognition is good for me, because it keeps me high in spirits. I use it to my advantage. When people say that I'm one of the best drummers in England, I think, 'Well, *they* think that, but *I* know different.' As far as the money's concerned, it helps me, as far as bettering myself. I can buy stereo equipment, vibes, timpani, and it costs money. So, if I've got money, it means I can buy the best equipment, and it means I can buy the best musical education, which is very important to me. So I've used the money as carefully as what I can. I try to live very simply, in actual fact, though I do have a considerable amount of money for, you know, what I am. I try and live very basic. I don't have many, many luxuries in life, because I'm into a simple life. I come from a working-class family, so I've never known any better. So, just because I've got it, it doesn't mean I'm going to flaunt it."

"Good, you're putting it away."

"Well, I have one thing which you would possibly call a luxury. I have a summer home. My reason for having a summer home—"

"In England?"

"It's in Spain, the Canary Islands. The reason for having it is that I tour *so* much that to take four weeks holiday and check into a hotel is crippling, you know? So, I figured I could get a cheap house out there, because property *is* so cheap, you know? I figured that would be something I would really want. If there was a luxury in life—I don't think musical instruments are a luxury; they're a necessity, it's like food, you know? That's what I call my luxury. If I have one."

"Where do you see yourself going in the immediate future?"

He hesitated, his back against the wall, then brought his knees up and rested his arms on them. Two couples maneuvered past us, going downstairs. We could hear a mellow clarinet solo from below.

"Keep on studying?" I asked. "Keep on learning?"

"Yes, I see myself studying, obviously carry on studying. It's very hard to say, you know? I'm not too sure of my own progress. All I can say is that I'm going to do the best I can. It's very hard. My main goal in life, as far as a musician is concerned, is obviously to be like the man BR, you know? I feel that I have to try to achieve *something* like he's done, and I have to achieve that same level of musicianship, but related to *writing* music. I also feel that to write music is one of the greatest things, as well. And I feel that drummers are limited, because on the drums you don't really play a melodic tune, there's no notes, so a drummer is sort of held back, as far as *writing* music is concerned. And I feel that learning tune percussion, such as the xylophone and the marimba and things like that, help me write. And I think this is important, to sort of have that *edge*, you know, to be in front. Because if you play piano, you can write your own music, and that's the greatest thing, to have freedom, total freedom in music, and play your own material. With percussion, with drums, unless you go on to *tune* percussion, you're restricted. And I'm sure Buddy would agree to that. I'm sure he can hum things and people can write them down, and I used to do it that way. I used to sing things into a tape recorder and then give them to a piano player and say, 'Write the notes down.' But now I can do it myself. And I can't tell you..."

"Buddy would've loved to do that."

"I'm sure he could, if he just sat down, but it takes time. I know he's a very impatient man." He laughed softly, and a warmth came into his voice. "But I love him because of that, because that kind of impatient thing that he puts across comes out in his playing. I mean, I can see it, you know? But it's controlled."

We talked for a while longer, then went back downstairs and joined the group. About 2:30, Buddy and I decided to walk back to the Hilton, which was quite a hike.

It was one of those pleasantly cool, foggy London nights in October, with sidewalks wet after rain, almost no traffic except the occasional, cheerful, red double-decker bus, brightly lighted and empty, casting its moving image on the black mirrored street, and a few shiny little cars humming along and, in the distance, a series of misty yellow halos around the streetlights. We walked down Regent Street, seeing our lonely reflections in the store windows, Buddy in a checkered topcoat, me in a sheepskin, then turned right on Piccadilly and headed for Park Lane. Our footsteps sounded hollow on the pavement and we could see our breath in the damp breeze from the Thames. I loved to walk in London at night and so did he.

"Had a long talk with Carl Palmer," I said.

"Yeah, I know."

"Didn't realize he was such a serious kid."

"I think it's a matter of simple dedication," he said very quietly. "I mean, granted, he's got superior abilities to begin with, but then he goes that extra mile that the others aren't willing to go. And it makes all the difference. He knows how to draw on the past, how to take advantage of what's gone down before him. You have a few superior people around today, but years ago you had people like Lester Young, you had Prez, you had Bird, you had Duke, you had so many people who were dedicated to the point of practically giving up their lives for their music. A guy like Carl understands the fact that he's got an opportunity to stand on the shoulders of giants like that. He's got the brains and he's musically hip enough to listen and *learn* from the old Basie things, Prez things, Lunceford things, and to grow from them. He's growing on what was laid down by all the other people, the people that I grew from, and he understands the value of that. See, you can't buy that knowledge and you've got to be humble enough to *want* to learn. I mean, when I came up in this business there was no such thing as a 'caste' system, man, no such thing as unapproachable millionaire superstar musicians. Hell, they used to be on the bandstand *after* a gig and stay all night. Jam sessions. You'd get up on a bandstand, it was lucky to get ten men on it, and you'd find *thirty* cats up there, playing thirty *kinds* of music, the same tune, but thirty different interpretations of it. Wild Bill Davidson would play his, Roy Eldridge would play his, Sweets would play his. Whole room would be swinging, then all the guys would be looking at the one guy who was playing the solo—you know, having a cigarette, having a joint, having a belt, whatever, but looking and *listening*. Today, man, you get five guys up on the bandstand to play, four of them are looking to take a *cab*. Music was our whole life back then, money or no money, it was what we lived for."

We were on the corner of New Bond Street and he stopped to look in the window of a store. His reflection in the glass was very clear, face tired and serious, coat collar turned up, hands shoved in his pockets. He looked at his face, blinked at it, and I remember the way his voice changed. I had to move closer to hear.

"I'm very lucky, you know? I've had some very lucky moments in my life. I don't usually get carried away when I talk about this shit, but, you know, great moments are great to you—or they become great—when you get an opportunity to know the people you think *will* be great. And I had the chance to play with them when they were young. I've had the honor and the pleasure of recording with Art Tatum, the greatest jazz piano player of all time. That has to be considered a great moment. To have recorded with Bird, *Charley Parker With Strings*, which turned out to be a collector's item, to be called to play on that date with Paul Standards and Ray Brown, I'd have to consider that one of the great moments. I'm part of that scene, so that's a great moment.

To have recorded with Hampton was a great moment." He glanced at me. "You were there, you were at that whole session."

"Sunday, September eighth," I said. "Bell Studios. I couldn't possibly forget that afternoon. Nobody who was there could possibly forget it. I'd never seen *or* heard anything like that before. And I don't think I've ever seen you happier than you were that day."

"I'll tell you something strange, man, and this is the God's honest truth, and I very seldom use that term. Just a few days after that recording session—I remember the date, September twelfth—Hampton was rushed to the hospital for massive internal bleeding. You remember that?"

"Very well."

"Rushed to Mount Siani Hospital. I went in to see him. Found out he nearly died before they got him there. It was his colon. Almost bled to death internally, it was down to a matter of minutes, that's how close he came. I looked at him in that hospital bed and I thought, 'Oh, God, no, not Hamp.' I mean, I came up with this guy, you know, he was part of what it was all about. And we almost lost him. I came out of that hospital and I found myself crying. But the strange thing was, I wasn't crying for Hamp, even though I love him and I would've done anything to help him, I wasn't really crying for him. I was crying for myself. It's something that starts happening to you at my age. You start to lose your friends, people you've come up with, worked with, laughed with, people who were part of your life. And they start to go, one by one, and you can't believe it. And there's never going to be anyone to replace them. They're just gone. And each time it happens, each time you get the telephone call or pick up the paper, the shock really gets to you. It gives you a new awareness of your own mortality, because you were part of that scene. And then you think, 'I never got to know them as well as I should have.' And it's too late. And they never really got to know me, because—well, I suppose, if I'm honest about it, I didn't let them. I don't really want to admit that to myself, because it's too painful, but I think it's true."

We started walking again, crossed New Bond Street, where we could see several pairs of headlights way off in the fog.

Buddy cleared his throat, tested it. "Remember that night in California when I told you that Marie and Cathy and my family didn't understand what I was all about?"

"Yes."

"Well, I've been thinking about it for almost a month now and I've decided to try something. I haven't changed my mind, but I've decided to try to get to know *them* better. Because, I thought, if I really do feel so terribly alone—and I do—maybe I can alleviate that if I stop thinking about it, and about myself, and try to get more interested in *them* again. If I give more than I've ever given before, you know? The thing is, I love them, I've always loved them. Let's face it, they didn't exactly get a bargain in me, in my personality, but they've stuck with me all the way. I mean, a wife who's loved me, in spite of all my assorted neuroses, for twenty-one years, and a beautiful daughter who loves me, and my father and brother and sisters, who've all loved me—and stuck by me, no matter what, when, or where. I don't know if it'll work, but I'm going to try again. Maybe it's a pipe dream. Maybe nobody really gets to understand anybody else. Maybe we really *are* in solitary confinement for life. But I'm going to dream the dream, man, because I don't think I can live without it. It's that simple. Maybe I'll blow it, but at least I'm going to try. I'm going to try again and I'll keep on trying and I know *they'll* try. And, who knows, maybe we'll break through to each other. If it isn't too late."

He stopped walking abruptly and stood there, looking up the street, frowning slightly, as if trying to remember something.

When he turned to me, his gaze went inward for just a moment, then focused on my eyes. I could see his breath in the air.

"I don't think it's too late," he said. "Do you?"

12

THE DECEMBER 1974 issue of *American Way*, the celebrated inflight magazine of American Airlines, with a readership of 2.7 million per month that year, devoted its cover story to Buddy Rich, Written by Mel Tormé, with a superb action cover shot by David Redfern and a total of eleven other color photographs throughout the seven-page article. There were feature articles in that issue by regular contributing writers Isaac Asimov, James Beard, Bob Considine, and Judith Crist, but the most letters to the editor concerned The Tormé piece, requesting more stories about the worldwide resurgence of jazz, particularly in major cities such as London, Paris, Rome, Frankfurt, Tokyo, Sydney, Melbourne, Boston, New York, Philadelphia, Chicago, New Orleans, San Francisco, and Los Angeles, where big and small jazz bands from many countries were on tour that year, playing to theaters that were sold out months in advance of their appearances.

As it happened, Buddy had heard about the cover story, of course, but hadn't read it until he flew American from New York to Los Angeles the first week in December. Following is Mel Tormé's story in its entirety:

BUDDY RICH: One of a Kind

Mel Tormé gives candid insights into the dazzling
talent of Buddy Rich, who is now spearheading the
phenomenal resurgence of jazz.

By MEL TORMÉ

One afternoon, back in 1940, I rather brazenly picked up
the telephone and called the Chicago Theatre, asking the
operator to connect me with Buddy Rich, Tommy Dorsey's
drummer. When Mr. Rich came on the line, I introduced
myself and tried glibly to pawn myself off as a friend of
Mickey Scrima's (Harry James's percussionist and a reputed
friend of Rich's).

I was lying through my teeth.

Such cheek might be forgivable, though, when one considers
that, at the ripe old age of fourteen, I could not walk past
Wurlitzer's or Lyon and Healy's on Wabash Avenue in the
Windy City without gawking at the drum displays in the
windows. I had begun my love affair with cymbals, tom-toms
and the like during my incarceration at Shakespeare Grammar
School on Chicago's south side, and had driven our neighbors
bananas, practicing on my first set of drums at all hours. My
loyalties shifted like the winds: Ray Bauduc was the best
drummer. No. It was Gene Krupa. No. Come to think of it,
Chick Webb easily surpassed both of them. Or did I mean
Dave Tough? Then I heard Buddy Rich and all my indecision
came to an abrupt halt.

From the moment I was exposed to his talent via Artie
Shaw's record of *Carioca*, I instinctively knew I had heard
drums played at their optimum, and that this blindingly gifted
performer's technique, taste, sense of dynamics, and his

uncanny grasp of what syncopation was all about, began
where every other drummer's ended.

Critics of his early work complained that he played too
loud, that his rim shots were intrusive, that he interfered with
horn soloists, that he undermined arrangements right and left.
But with that omniscient wisdom inherent in fourteen-year-
olds, I knew they were dead wrong. Buddy Rich was,
indisputably, the greatest drummer ever, and I had to tell him
so—on the telephone, at least.

He was polite, but abrupt, that day back in 1940. He
thanked me, told me to say "hello" to Scrima when I saw him
again (I suspect he knew I had never met Mickey) and hung up.

We never actually met until 1945. In the interim, he had
made some kind of history not only with the Tommy Dorsey
juggernaut but ultimately with the U.S. Marines, where he set
some kind of record for insubordination and time spent in the
brig, despite his value as a judo instructor.

A freshly discharged BR sauntered into the Palladium
Ballroom in Hollywood one Evening in '45, still wearing his
Marine "greens" and sporting the shortest haircut in tonsorial
memory. He had not had a pair of drumsticks in his hands for
over six months. The resident bandleader, Charlie Spivak,
spotted Rich, introduced him to the audience and invited him
to "sit in" with the band on *Hawaiian War Chant*. Spivak's
drummer, Bobby Rickey, handed Buddy the sticks somewhat
reluctantly and the erstwhile judo instructor proceeded to stun
the crowd with an incredible percussive tour de force. He had
never heard the arrangement before, yet, with that amazing
built-in radar unit he was born with, he caught the brass
punctuations and the sax nuances as though he had personally
authored the chart.

When the ovation he received finally subsided, he stood, bowed mockingly, one arm behind his back, one across his stomach, like a six-year-old lad reciting a poem, and handed the sticks back to Rickey with an offhand, "Here, kid." Bobby, at that precise moment, looked as if he would like to pursue another line of work.

I had heard of Rich's legendary fracas with Sinatra at the Astor; I was well aware of the fact that he was mainly unapproachable, an iconoclast, who, it was said, bordered on the antisocial. Still, I was so moved by his work that night, I made it my business to meet him.

To my surprise and delight, he was warm, friendly, and had actually heard of me and my then—vocal group, the Mel-Tones. Almost at once, we became inseparable. He rejoined the Dorsey band and he would pick me up every night at my folks' apartment in his immaculate yellow Lincoln Continental. (BR has always been a car freak, and in those days he had an overwhelming predilection for Continentals.) We would head out to the Casino Gardens, the Dorsey-owned ballroom at the beach, and I would plunk myself down on the bandstand, near Buddy, and watch, open-jawed and disbelieving, the impossible combination of hands and feet he would put together of an evening. I always likened him to the best athletes I had ever seen: impeccable form, flawless technique and an ability to think and act with mind-boggling speed and accuracy.

He used to like *The Touch of Your Hand* and sometimes, as I sang it, he would become morose and confide to me that he was still hurting from his haunting love affair with Lana Turner, at the same time staring pensively at the slim gold bracelet-watch she had given him, inscribed: "Time for you always. L."

He was champing at the bit to form his own band; Dorsey said he could have his release when and if he (Buddy) could come up with a replacement that suited him (Tommy).

When the Dorsey band appeared on the Fitch Bandwagon with Dick Powell as host and the Mel-Tones and me as regulars, Buddy and bass-player Sandy Block set me up. First, Rich just disappeared and Tommy irascibly began cursing and storming. How the hell were they to rehearse without a drummer? Sandy innocently suggested that I "sit in," just to keep time. TD agreed, grumpily, and we played *Opus One* and *Sunny Side of the Street*, both of which I knew like the back of my hand.

Surprise! Dorsey liked my playing. Buddy's ploy had worked and suddenly Mr. D began calling me on a daily basis, offering me Rich's drum chair in the band, probably the most flattering proposal I ever received.

What Tommy did not know was that the more I watched Buddy play, the more convinced I was of a lusterless future for me at the drums. It had always been my ambition to be a drumming bandleader. Now, after my privileged relationship with the greatest of all drummers, I became determined to pursue a singing career.

Buddy finally obtained his release from TD and formed his own band. In 1947, we found ourselves in New York, Buddy breaking his back to gain recognition and popularity for his orchestra; me, in the midst of all that bobbysox "Velvet Fog" garbage. Once again, our friendship thrived. I saw, fell in love with, and promptly bought one of the first five postwar MG-TCs delivered to this country. Not to be outdone, BR bought one of the remaining ones.

We drove them out to the Meadowbrook in New Jersey one rain-drenched night and proudly displayed them, side by side, in the parking lot. We dated a lot of lovely ladies. We heard a lot of music up and down and across the length and breath of Manhattan.

In 1949, we appeared together for the first time at the Paramount in New York and there was Trouble in Paradise. The band's fortunes had not fared well; payroll days were tenuous at best. At the first rehearsal, I noticed a few extra drum cartons and when I casually asked about them, he snapped: "Louie Bellson better learn how to play *one* bass before he tries two." I was surprised at this outburst because Buddy had always praised Bellson, both as a drummer and as a guy. (If there is a nicer, less abrasive man living than Louie Bellson, you've got to prove it to me.)

At any rate, Buddy broke open the cartons to reveal a pair of twenty-inch bass drums; the next day, opening day, he tore the audience to shreds by playing his principal solo (*Old Man River*) at breakneck speed on those two bass drums. Period. No cymbals, tom-toms or snare drum. He simply sat behind two bass drums and played an astonishing solo with his feet! (Well, not so astonishing when one considers that Rich was one of the best tap-dancers around.) I closed that show, and believe me, after *Old Man River*, it took me the best part of ten of my twenty-five allotted minutes to recapture the audience.

I finally found out that Rich's rancor about Bellson had nothing whatsoever to do with Louie. It was merely exasperation on Buddy's part that a mindless and fickle public as well as a plethora of jazz critics were extolling Bellson's innovative twin-bass drum venture when it was so patently obvious that Rich played more with one foot than anyone could possibly play with three. (Had everyone forgotten his incredible performance with his old band, when he had broken his left wrist and played the entire show with only one hand?)

I came to realize that Buddy's whole life had been a series of challenges and that he enjoyed meeting these tests. There is something singularly heroic about accepting the thrown gauntlet and emerging triumphant to the crowd's roar. It is a way of life with Buddy Rich and the music world was never more aware of it than on that fateful night at the Newport Jazz Festival in 1967 when, during a mass "drum-in," after everyone had played themselves out, the Master took the stage and gave a virtuoso performance that lasted over twenty minutes. At the end of the solo, which Rich reckons as the apex of his career, he simply threw the sticks in the air, got up and walked away. He had "said" all there was to say behind a set of drums. Comment of any kind would have been redundant.

While he and I broke it up at the Paramount, our friendship unraveled a bit and became somewhat tattered due to childishness and petulance on both our parts (although Buddy will staunchly maintain I was the solitary culprit). At any rate, we were not as close after that as we had been; a short time later, he broke up the band and became an itinerant musician once more.

Restlessly, he jumped from "Jazz at the Philharmonic" to director of music for Josephine Baker to the featured drum chair with Harry James. He put another band together in the late '60s and appeared on a summer TV series.

At one point, after a scarifying heart attack, he was convinced he would never play drums again; it was a singing career he wanted. We had become very friendly once more (our whole pal-ship has been on-again-off-again for years) and he asked me to come and hear him in New York's Living Room. He was, as always, delightful to listen to, with that slightly rough edge to his voice, the infectious grin, the careful attention to lyrics (no doubt instilled in him by another on-again-off-again buddy, Frank Sinatra). But, God! The world's greatest drummer committed to a life of competing with a parade of crooners in a string of upholstered sewers across these great United States of ours?!

One night, while he was appearing at the Living Room, we wandered, after his last show, onto Fifty-second Street. It was a rainy night and "The Street" wasn't what it had once been anyway. Progressive jazz had foisted itself upon the public; the mass audience, as well as the more discerning few, had pondered the incomprehensibility of "be-bop" and were staying away in droves.

We poked our heads into the Onyx or the Three Deuces or the Famous Door—I forget which— to hear the sound of Allan Eager's tenor sax wafting across the bar. Buddy wanted to leave; he seemed low and disconsolate. I persuaded him to stay and listen a while. Eager, backed by a rhythm section that included the then-king of "bop" drummers, Max Roach, was working hard to see how many notes he could cram into a single bar—a bid, no doubt, for a niche in the *Guinness Book of World Records*. Max, whom I have since come to appreciate and respect, was, at that time, dedicated to the proposition that all bass drums are to be played only on rare occasion—a "tap" here and a "boom" there. The result was one continuous sheet of cymbal overtone that had me fighting to discover where "two" and "four" were. (Hell, "one" and "three" as well, when you get right down to it.)

Buddy sat there, looking more depressed and dejected by the minute. Several times, he scowled at me and muttered, "Let's get the hell out of here." Finally, I nodded, and as we made to leave, Eager acknowledged our presence, which elicited half-hearted applause from the handful of customers present. Then he asked Buddy to play a tune with the group.

Buddy shook his head and growled, "No, man, I don't want to play," but Eager kept insisting (goading, I thought) and his taunting attitude jangled my nerve-ends. Allan always had somewhat of a reputation as a smart-ass, and what I was reading into his attitude was, "Hey, old-timer, come on up and make a jerk of yourself. Let everyone see how corny you sound after hearing Max Roach."

Allan, you dummy! Didn't you realize you had just flung the gauntlet of combat into the face of one of the true gauntlet-chewers of all time?

Buddy, who had not played in months (shades of that evening at the Palladium in '45), slowly walked onto the stand. The drums were rudimentary, not a full set, and they were tuned to simulate wet plastic bags, slightly filled with water.

Eager smirked at Max, who had taken a seat near me along the wall, and kicked off *I Found a New Baby* at an absurd tempo that bordered on "one" instead of "four/four."

And Buddy Rich played.

After backing Eager's solos superbly, he embarked on what I can only describe as one of the God-damnedest drum solos in the history of the instrument. No, it was more than a solo. It was a composition that embodied the finest elements of form. There was an "A," a "B" and a "C" to it, fully orchestrated on the various component parts of that drum set—carefully, lovingly developed, flawlessly accomplished. As I looked around, I saw people beginning to pour into the place. Someone had spread the word quickly that Buddy Rich was playing drums again, and so help me, just like in some lousy, late-late show "B" movie, that club was suddenly overflowing with bodies.

I sneaked a look at Max. His jaw was actually dropped, his mouth open, his head shaking plainly from side to side in disbelief. I wasn't present to hear Buddy's highly acclaimed Newport triumph, but I cannot conceive of its being better than what I was privileged to hear that night on Fifty-second Street. When he finished, he was treated to the most riotous standing ovation I have ever witnessed. In typical Rich fashion, he underplayed his response to the tribute, adopting a somber look and merely nodding his acknowledgment.

As he made his way along the bar, accepting the handshakes, the pounding on the back, the smiles and—believe it or not—a few tears of appreciation, he could not suppress a self-satisfied smile. He shot a glance at me and I jerked my head back in the direction of the stand.

Allan Eager was genuinely whistling and applauding as vociferously as anyone. So was Max Roach. That evening put an end to Buddy's singing career.

Since that time, he has acquired the widespread fame he always deserved. His record-breaking big band, best-selling LPs, and numerous appearances on the *Tonight* show have made Buddy Rich a household name. Which is not to say that fame of that kind has made him any less obstreperous or cantankerous. If anything, he is more opinionated, more aggressive, less tolerant of people's foibles than ever—and if I wrote anything else, he would doubtless damn me as a phony, gutless, sugar-coating jerk.

So, in his own words, I have to tell it "straight life." I suspect our friendship is better and stronger than ever, predicated on years of not talking to one another, followed by years of closeness, followed by years of not talking to one another, etc.

Maybe the reason BR and I will always remain close friends is *our* similar backgrounds. We both began performing at extremely tender ages. Buddy, at five, and billed as "Traps, the Drum Wonder," toured Australia as the star of a variety review. I began singing with famous bands around Chicago at approximately the same age. We have both followed our stars wherever they led us and have managed to survive and proliferate in a business in which talent is not always the key ingredient for success—and can often be a detrimental factor.

Buddy Rich always believed in himself and that self-faith and determination have seen him through hard times—not necessarily financially, but career-wise. Now, with his image firmly implanted on the public psyche and his New York night club, Buddy's Place, thriving, it looks like he can relax and enjoy his life from here on in. It's about time, OOAK. (That's what I call him, OOAK.) One of a kind.

In July, 1991, four years after Buddy's death, Mel Tormé published a well-received biography, *Traps the Drum Wonder: The Life of Buddy Rich*, originally released by Oxford University Press, and named as a "New York Times Notable Book of the Year." The work was reissued in 1998 in both hard and soft cover by Rebeats Press (230 pages with 30 halftones). Johnny Carson called the book "An honest, loving portrait of a genius."

Tormé also published five other books, including *The Other Side of the Rainbow* (1970), and an autobiography, *It Wasn't All Velvet* (1988). He was the recipient of two Grammy awards for Best Male Jazz Vocal Performance, 1983 and 1984.

Mel Tormé died in 1999 at the age of seventy-four.

Afterword

THE FOLLOWING YEAR, several significant events occurred that would alter Buddy's life. Due to the popularity of the first Buddy's Place, the decision was made to close the club at Second Avenue and Sixty-fourth Street and move into a plush new Buddy's Place in April, 1975, a lavishly appointed, 400-seat downstairs facility in Marty's Bum Steer II restaurant, 133 West Thirty-third Street, directly across from the Statler Hilton Hotel, in the Madison Square Garden area. Because of the size of the new club (twice as large as the first one), Buddy decided to break up his small band and form a sixteen-piece big band composed almost entirely of very young musicians. Next, to keep the place filled, he initiated a policy of offering a name singer and/or comedian on every bill. His new European concert tour, scheduled for April, with Lionel Hampton, Teddy Wilson, and George Duvivier, was cancelled. Opening night for the new club was set for April 28, and Nipsey Russell and Carmen McRae were signed as the first headliners with the big band.

The build-up was extensive and the press was alert to the fact that the new Buddy's Place was undoubtedly the most expensive and ambitious jazz club to open in New York in thirty years; the design and furnishings alone were estimated to cost in excess of $400,000. Where did that kind of money come from, especially in the recession economy of 1975? Most of it was financed by Martin Ross, a slim, youthful-looking ex-stockbroker, who was then thirty-eight. As a partner at Charles Plohn & Company, he was earning more than $200,000 a year by 1969, when the bull market turned bearish and his income fell sharply for the next three years. In October, 1972, Ross quit the brokerage business and, four months later, opened the first Marty's Bum Steer steak house on East Seventy-third Street. After a single year, the place was doing a volume of close to $1 million, and he was ready to open a second restaurant, this time in combination with the proven drawing capability of Buddy's Place, which would be located just downstairs.

I remember opening night vividly. There was an elaborate press reception several hours before the sold-out first show, and the only part of the decor that wasn't finished on time was the covering of the canopy out front. You entered through heavy glass doors into a foyer with glass walls, revealing enormous blowups of Buddy in a glass display case above the carpeted stairway, with smaller pictures of Nipsey Russell and Carmen McRae, and even Mel Tormé, who would be the next attraction with the band, May 12–24. A second set of glass doors, to the right, opened on a carpeted hallway leading to the restaurant, with a bar area just outside, and the club itself was entered through a final set of glass doors across the hall from the bar.

I arrived a little late, and as I walked down the open stairway, flanked by ferns, I was surprised by the size of the press crowd; an estimate the next day listed the number at 450, but it was a conservative guess, in my opinion, because all of the 400 seats were occupied and even standing room became very congested. Some stood in line at the long buffet tables, others filled the 200 candle-lit tables, photographers and television crews set up their equipment around the four mirrored pillars, and there was a line waiting to get into the glass-enclosed cocktail lounge and bar, of course, because the waiters and waitresses were swamped with booze orders from the tables. Even the raised and roped-off VIP area in back was crowded, mostly by photographers trying to set up shots of the entire room. Nobody was on the bandstand yet, but the heavy stage lights around the ceiling were trained on fifteen "BR" music stands, and the white marine pearl sparkled like new, along with the frames of Buddy's drums, which also looked new. I made my way through the crowd to the bandstand, where there was still a little room, because a crew of sound technicians had cleared space to set up ladders as they adjusted the three gigantic speakers of the special sound system.

Buddy finally came out with the band at seven o'clock sharp, just an hour before the show, which was scheduled for an especially early start because of the opening-night reviewers. He looked almost skinny in a dark-blue turtleneck and gray trousers, and his gold "dog-tag" pendant and chain caught the light with every move as he adjusted the microphone. The one common denominator you couldn't help noticing about the other fifteen musicians, as they took their places, was their predominately youthful appearance; most were in their twenties. Trumpets occupied the top row: Lloyd Michels (lead), Richard Hurwitz, Ross Konikoff, and Danny Hayes. To the left of Buddy's slot in the middle row was Ben Brown on bass, then trombones to the right: Barry Maur (lead), Gerald Chamberlain and Anthony Salvatori (bass). In front, Greg Kogan was on piano, Wayne Wright played a left-handed guitar, and saxophones were to the right: Peter Yellin (lead alto), Bill Blaut (alto), Steve Marcus (soprano and tenor), Bob Mintzer (tenor), and Roger Rosenberg (baritone).

Buddy tapped on the microphone. "Okay, hold it down, please. We want you to continue to eat and drink and enjoy yourselves, but we've been asked to audition the band for all of you folks, to see if we can stay for the second show." He waited a beat for the start of the laughter, then broke into it: "So we're going to play a couple of tunes and give you an idea of what's going to happen down here for the next—fifty or sixty years." He extended his right arm to the bandstand. "This is my band and I'm the drummer." Applause started, but he interrupted it: "Oh, no applause, no applause; you'll get the tab on the way *out.*" This time, he waited for the laughter to end. "We're going to play about four or five tunes for you. All we ask is that you don't get up and *dance.*"

Buddy hopped up to his place in the middle row, gave a loud verbal downbeat, and they blasted into a brassy *On Broadway*, *Pieces of Dreams*, and *Ease On Down the Road*, all of which would later be included in their first album, *Big Band Machine*, for Groove Merchant. The new sound system was superb.

Nipsey Russell was introduced, came on in a dark silk jacket, white tie and shirt, and immediately launched into one of his "pomes":

"Don't buy a waterbed for the baby,
Or things will be very grim;
You'll never know if he's wetting the *bed*,
Or the bed is wetting *him*!"

I remember the way Nipsey laughed the loudest of all, a trick he used occasionally to loosen up a crowd, and it worked. He gave them one more taste before stepping down:

"As I was sitting home looking out the window of my apartment on Park Avenue…Park Avenue and One Hundred Thirty-second Street, I said, 'This is going to be a great night in New York, a great city, the only place in the world you can walk into an Arab home in a Scandinavian neighborhood and find a Puerto Rican baby eating motsaballs with chopsticks.' And there is crime, as we know, there is crime. In my neighborhood, a guy stuck up a bank and got mugged before he could reach the getaway car. But, I say, we're going to add a new element to that scene here, and it's going to be Buddy's Place, a place of music and merriment. You just saw a sample and tonight we're going to turn it all loose. So, come down and be with us, and if you can't come, just send the money and we'll understand."

Buddy's dressing room was located on the same floor, to the right of the bandstand, and could be entered from the hall or the bandstand itself. It was at least twice as large as the one in the old club, but seemed even bigger because of a floor-to-ceiling mirror on the far wall. Most of the space was devoted to a rectangular "living room" and the actual dressing room was separated by a louvered door. Tan was the dominant color, from dark pine-paneled walls and teakwood cabinets to fitted carpeting, and most of the modern furniture was arranged around a thick glass coffee table with heavy chrome legs. Glass corner tables held graceful vases of flowers, befitting an opening night, the bar was well-stocked, bottles of champagne cooled in silver ice buckets, and the stereo played softly.

About half an hour before the first show, Buddy's entire family started arriving: Mag and Jo from California, Bob and Louise, Mickey, Marie, and Cathy. It was the first time I had ever seen them all together, and I was given a rare glimpse into the nonstop banter and scalpel-sharp sarcasm of a family that seemed unusually close and vitally interested in each other, despite the unusually wide age gaps. Bob Rich never stopped smiling, wearing a smart new two-button gray suit and a new striped tie, leaning forward to catch every word, having a hell of a time. It made me feel happy to watch him.

When the conversation turned to Cathy, it was all about her first record, to be released the next day on the Groove Merchant label, with a press conference at the club. Titled *Roxie*, it was by "Cathy and the Richettes," a new group she had formed, and it was from the Broadway show *Chicago*, a musical vaudeville, which would open May 15, starring Gwen Verdon, Chita Rivera, and Jerry Orbach.

Buddy stuck the forty-five record on the stereo, turned the volume up slightly, and told everybody to shut up and listen. Cathy sat next to Marie on the long couch, stared fixedly at the carpet for the first few bars, then glanced up, excited and lovely in a long white dress with short sleeves, almost no makeup, and her dark hair lustrous in a new short style. Several months before, she had moved out of her parents' apartment, an inevitable decision that Buddy and Marie accepted with resignation, finally, although it was very difficult, and the transition had been painful for all of them. But Cathy seemed to be "getting her act together," as Buddy put it, in many more ways than one. Watching her that night, after not seeing her for some time, my mind kept returning to the old club and to the rather awkward youngster in the wild denim out-fits, singing with her first group, moving to the music, snapping her fingers, off on a trip. It had been only ten months ago, but when a girl reaches her very early twenties, the rate of physical and emotional change often accelerates dramatically, and the girl in the long white dress and short hair seemed something of a stranger to me. Yet the change was fascinating and pleasant, and when the record ended and the room ignited with applause and cheers, Cathy's eyes and voice and all-out laughter were the same as always, and time stood still for just a moment. Buddy turned to the flip side, and Marie took Cathy's hand as we listened to *Sugartime Medley*.

I enjoyed the flip side almost as much as the title song, but *Roxie* was already being given pre-release attention by disk-jockeys, undoubtedly because of the tremendous build-up for *Chicago*, which was predicted to be a smash hit. Buddy also had a new forty-five record out, *The Bull* (flip side, *Nik-Nik*), his first single with the big band, but when somebody asked to hear it, he carefully side-stepped the request, not wanting to detract from Cathy's big moment, and I thought he handled it superbly.

Leo poured some champagne then, and Sandi and Stanley came in to say that the house was almost packed and there was a line of couples all the way upstairs waiting to be seated. Stanley, who had recently signed a contract to manage the club, went around the room to shake hands with everybody, and Sandi was right at his side, looking super in a new cream-colored evening dress with a matching turban that accentuated her tan.

A few minutes later, my wife Verity arrived, straight from the Pan Am office, where she had to attend a late meeting. Although I knew she felt out of place in a simple, dark, tailored outfit, she looked great to me.

"Buddy handed her a glass of champagne, "Saved this for you, Verity, glad you could make it, how about a dance?"

"Love it." She took a sip, gave me the glass, and did several fast steps with him, a very slim girl, her face oval and gentle, with large brown eyes.

"Heavy date tonight?" he asked, walking back.

She laughed in the sudden, spontaneous way that Buddy could make her laugh; they had an almost identical sense of dry humor. She had looked forward to that evening, and her dark hair was holding reasonably well after such a long day at work, ends brushing the corners of her lips.

Finally, it was time for the show. Bob and Louise, Mag, Jo, and Mickey sat at tables down front, and Verity and I joined Marie, Sandi, and Cathy in the VIP section at the back of the room. Waitresses hurried to and from the tables, trying to fill orders before the houselights were dimmed. I remember the sudden hush and the air of anticipation as the band took the stand. And the feel of the place when they were into the first number, with the audience in semidarkness except for the hundreds of candles.

And the happy faces of Marie and Cathy, sitting close to each other, looking very much alike in that soft light.

There were reviews in all of the papers the next day, and even television reviews, with good footage taken at the press reception, including interviews with Buddy, but I think the most objective and comprehensive review appeared in *Variety*, April 30, 1975:

Buddy's Place, N.Y.
Buddy Rich Orch. (16), Carmen McRae,
Nipsey Russell; $6, $8 cover.

The second edition of Buddy's Place is probably the most ambitious cafe to be opened in New York since World War II. It's a 400-seater with a superb sound system and a policy which pro—vides three headliners on every bill. The spot is downstairs in a new restaurant in the Madison Square Garden area, Marty's Bum Steer II, operated separately.

The present bill, with Buddy Rich's new 16-piece band, Carmen McRae and Nipsey Russell, is reminiscent of the bright days of the long-gone Paramount Theatre. All that is missing is the rising stage. They all act like headliners on this show and each did a full act opening night. Result was a marathon that ran for more than two hours. Naturally, the show will have to be cut.

Rich has a big and lovely sound. The king-sized complement of men, comprising four trumpets, three trombones, five reeds and three rhythms, along with Rich's drums, are instrumental in producing power and light. There's a sunny feeling. Rich modestly declines a vast number of solos which would again mark him as the best in his field. Instead, his beat gives the orchestra a driving rhythm and a solid bottom. There were more solos when he headed his former six-piece crew at the old spot, and they are missed.

Russell is indeed a funny man. His "pomes" strike a pleasurable note and his lines, many of which have been used by him previously, sound as fresh as when first heard. He also provides a bit of dancing and the net result is one of potent entertainment.

McRae is also one of the major stars of this show. She has an interesting and sometimes sensitive voice which she can load with power when necessary. Her tunes are generally from the pre-1940 catalog, a great era in the Tin Pan Alley trade. The audience is able to catch her individualistic application on the tunes. Unfortunately, many of her arias are over-ornamented. The trick effects, while calling attention to the singer, often violate the spirit of the tune. How—ever, when she makes her simpler and unadorned statements, there is a sensitivity and much to commend. McRae was the major victim of the time overload. The audience was restive at that point and even the return of Galli-Curci would have made little difference.

The room seems to have an excellent future, even with mirrored pillars that block visibility from many seats. Virtually everything also has been done to make this an attractive and worthwhile entertainment project which deserves support. Besides, with many of the top rooms bowing out for the summer, this should be one of the few games in town.—*Jose.*

Several nights later, one of Buddy's oldest friends, Count Basie, came to the club. I had met Basie the previous September, when he celebrated his seventieth birthday with a party in the Grand Ballroom of the Waldorf Astoria. It was attended by more than 700 people, probably half of whom were musicians, but when

Basie took the stage after dinner with his seventeen-piece band, he only asked one musician in the audience to come up and join him. I remember the way he announced it: "You'll note I've asked Buddy Rich to sit in at the drums; he's my other son."

They didn't see each other often, because Basie was on the road with the band forty weeks a year, and had moved to the Bahamas in 1971, but Buddy still referred to him as "my other father," and meant it.

So when the Count showed up at the club, unannounced, and came to the dressing room before the show, Buddy was really ecstatic. They sat and talked about everything from one-nighters, which Basie was still playing, to the news that Mel Tormé had replaced Butch Miles with Don Osborne, the twenty-one-year-old drummer we had met at Mr. Kelly's last August, and that Miles had just joined Basie's band.

"How's Butch like the one-nighters?" Buddy asked.

Basie stroked his white muttonchops, smiled with the savvy of more than fifty years on the road. "He'll get used to it."

"Yeah, I know. After nine thousand years."

They both laughed softly and Basie unwrapped one of his familiar, fat cigars. "Hear you're going to South Africa."

Buddy nodded. "Signed for a week in Johannesburg, starting August fourth, then a week in Cape Town and Durban."

"The whole band?"

"Oh, yeah."

"You got a black bass player—what's his name?"

"Ben Brown. Twenty-one years old. Dynamite."

Basie lit his cigar slowly, turning it, smoke obscuring his face. "South African government has to issue him a work permit."

"No problem."

"They give him a work permit?"

"Not yet. Promoter says it's no problem."

Basie inspected his cigar, turned it in his fingers. "They'll give him a tourist visa, but you might have trouble on a work permit."

In the pause, Buddy sat forward stiffly, shoulders hunched. "If Brown doesn't work, nobody works. We made that as clear as you can make it, right from the beginning. I'll cancel the whole tour. I'll tell them to stick the tour up their ass. Nobody tells me who I can have in my band, here or there. *Nobody* tells me that."

Basie glanced at him, smiled. "You sure haven't changed any."

"I'll never change on that issue. Not after all these years. You know that. The musicians come first, then the audience, then, maybe, the government. If there's anything left."

I remember the way he said it, in the rapid staccato that almost always signaled the kind of interior screaming he thought no one could hear, and the moment is frozen in my mind for a number of reasons. Less than two months later, the South African govern-ment tacitly refused to issue Ben Brown a work permit, by offering him a tourist visa, making him a guest of the country, and suggesting that Buddy might replace him with a white bass player. After nine days of heated telephone calls, Buddy called a press conference at the club on July 17, and cancelled the entire tour. By the next day, the story broke in the worldwide news media, and the South African government denied responsibility for the problem, blaming the promoter, as usual. No one was deceived, least of all the press.

Anyway, that particular night at the club, Basie stayed and talked right up until show time, and when we finally walked out into the crowded room, he gave Buddy the usual bear-hug, then stood against the side wall with me as the band took their places and the crowd settled down.

"You a friend of his?" Basie asked quietly.

"Yes."

He nodded, watched Buddy stop at a front table to greet some people before taking the stand.

"Take a good look at the man," he said. "He'll probably be around as long as me, maybe longer. But just in case he isn't, take a good look, and don't forget what you saw."

Bibliography

Balliett, Whitney. *Super-Drummer: A Profile of Buddy Rich*. New York, The Bobbs-Merrill Co., 1968.

Meriwether, Doug. *The Buddy Rich Orchestra and Small Groups*. Spotswood, New Jersey: Joyce Music Publications, 1974.

_____, and Hintze, Clarence. *Mister, I Am the Band: Buddy Rich, His Life and Travels*. New York: Hal Leonard Publishing Corp., 1988.

Nesbitt, Jim. *Inside Buddy Rich*. New York: Kendor Music, 1984.

Rich, Buddy; Adler, Henri; Klickmann, F. Henri. *Buddy Rich's Modern Interpretation of Snare Drum Rudiments*. New York: Music Sales Corp., 1997.

_____. *Buddy Rich: Jazz Legend 1917-1987: Transcriptions and Analysis of the World's Greatest Drummer*. New York: Warner Bros. Publications, 1997.

Tormé, Mel. *Traps the Drum Wonder: The Life of Buddy Rich*. New York: Rebeats Press, 1998.

Periodicals

Newsweek. "New York Jazz Festival." July 9, 1974.

Tesser, Neil. "Buddy Rich Opens Club in New York." *The Chicago Sun-Times*, August 10, 1974.

Tormé, Mel. "Buddy Rich: One of a Kind." *American Way*, December, 1974.

Toronto Star, The. "Lawrence Welk (gasp) planning to jazz it up." October 23, 1974.

Variety. "Buddy's Place, N.Y." April 30, 1975.

Weisman, Steven R. "One Mel Swoop." *The New York Times,* September 13, 1974.

Welch, Chris. "Big Bad Buddy Rich Is Back." *Melody Maker* (London), October 23, 1974.

Index

"Traps, the Drum Wonder" at age two, in parents' vaudeville act, circa 1919.

Buddy's big band in early 1950s, appearing at New
York's famed Paramount Theater. As usual, he
surrounded himself with giants of the jazz world,
including Zoot Sims, tenor; Sweets Edison, trumpet;
Kai Winding, trombone.

Buddy's big band playing "uptown" at the Apollo
Theater, Harlem, New York, in the early 1950s.

All-star jam session in early 1940s (left to right): Count Basie, Lionel Hampton, Illinois Jacquet, Tommy Dorsey, Artie Shaw, Ziggy Elman, Buddy Rich, Les Paul, as they appeared on *Command Performance*, the show shortwaved by CBS to boys overseas.

While with the Dorsey band, Buddy roomed with Frank Sinatra, and, although their feuds sometimes made headlines, it was Sinatra who backed Buddy's first band after they both left Dorsey. Over the years, they remained close friends.

FRIENDS

Frequent guests at Buddy's Place included Artie Shaw (left), celebrated bandleader, clarinetist, producer, and author; and Sy Oliver, who worked with Buddy to change the style of the Dorsey band from Dixieland to Swing. *Photo by S. Kaplan.*

Buddy raps with Bobby Columby, drummer with
"Blood, Sweat and Tears."
Photo by Peter Lanzarone.

Heavyweight champion Joe Louis, one of Buddy's heros, at Birdland, circa 1940. Stanley Kay, a drummer in Buddy's band (and later his manager), looks on.

A private moment between Buddy and one of his closest friends, Gene Krupa, at 1974 party in New York given by top drummers to honor Krupa.

Jerry Lewis (a pretty good amateur drummer) joined in tribute to Krupa.

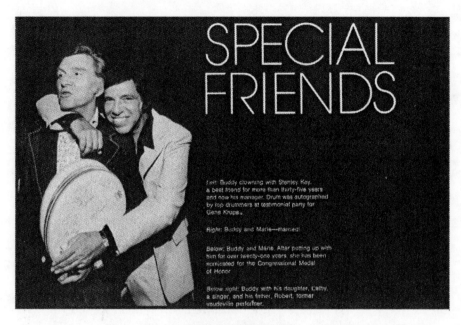

SPECIAL FRIENDS

Buddy clowning with Stanley Kay, his special friend and manager for more than 40 years. Drum was autographed by top drummers at testimonial party for Gene Krupa.

Photo by Peter Lanzarone.

SPECIAL FRIENDS
Buddy and Marie.

After 11 years of study, Buddy finally earned the coveted
black belt first degree in karate.
Photo by Russel C. Turiak.

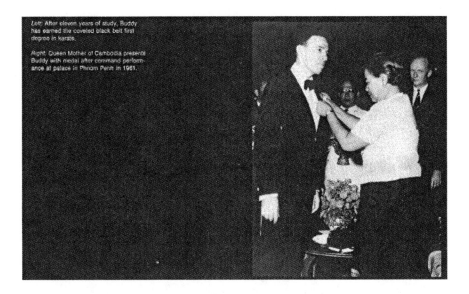

Queen Mother of Cambodia presents Buddy with medal after command performance in Phnom Penh, 1961.

Buddy's favorite club in Chicago.
Photo by John Minahan.

Buddy's first club in New York, 1974, was invariably packed, audiences tended to be young, and his solos never failed to bring the house down.
Photo by John Minahan.

Lional Hampton with Buddy at recording session at Bell
Studios in New York, September 8, 1974.
Photo by John Minahan.

On set of *The Tonight Show*, September 15, 1974, with close friend Johnny Carson and another frequent guest, Orson Bean.
Photo by John Minahan.

In Edinburgh, October 26, 1974, Buddy threw his tough-guy image to the Scottish winds and surprised a sold-out Usher Hall by walking on stage in a red Stuart kilt. He told the audience: "To be honest about it, I was a little scared to perform in drag, but, really, this is cool as hell, especially when I sit down."
Photo by John Minahan.

October 28, 1975, opening night at the new Buddy's Place, a plush 400-seat facility at 133 West 33rd Street, in the Madison Square Garden area, the most expensive and ambitious jazz club to open in New York since World War II.
Photo by John Minahan.

Cathy and Marie enjoy opening night. The following morning, Cathy released her first LP record, *Roxie*, by "Cathy and the Richettes," on the Groove Merchant label. *Photo by John Minahan.*

The whole Rich clan on opening night (left to right): sisters Marge and Jo, brother Mickey, Buddy, father Bob (then 87), stepmother Louise.
Photo by John Minahan.

CPSIA information can be obtained at www.ICGtesting.com
Printed in the USA
LVOW081536150412

277693LV00002B/68/A